A VIRGIN ON THE ARIZONA TRAIL

The Trials of a Tenderfoot

Jeremy Bolam

Tenderfoot n. Slang for an inexperienced person, particularly one who is not adapted to a rural or outdoor setting.

Acknowledgements

Thank you to all the great Americans who helped me along the trail with their open-hearted friendliness and generosity of spirit. Most of them get a mention somewhere in the text but a special mention should go to Lionel Joyce, Pop C and Li Brannfors, who really went the extra mile.

To Chris Townsend who walked the trail in 2002 and patiently responded to my naïve questions about the kit I should take with me.

To all the really helpful people at the Arizona Trail Association who provided me with some great information on the trail and quite rightly told me I was setting off too early in the year. My apologies in advance if I am less than complimentary about a few parts of the trail.

To Gill for not making a fuss when I told her I would be disappearing into the wilderness for 40 days, for keeping Holly Lodge going whilst I was away and for proof reading my ramblings.

To Chris Rheinberg for his considerable help in converting my manuscript and photos into the book you have in your hands and to Jo Lincoln for turning my maps into something worth looking at.

I do hope that you enjoy reading this book as much as I have enjoyed writing it. Poring over my trail notes and maps has helped me to relive every day of the journey all over again, which has been great fun. Memories of every inch I walked have come flooding back, but without the considerable pain of actually doing it.

Also, in these days of cheap books in every supermarket and great offers from online sellers, can I apologise if you have paid a bit more for this than you might have liked? I have published it myself through Create Space and decided to put colour photographs in so that if you don't like my writing, at least you have some pictures to look at. That has added considerably to the cost but I hope it will add to the enjoyment as well.

If a few copies are sold and a small profit is made, it will be split between the two causes that I raised a little money for on the way, Edith Creasey and the Friends of St Andrews, Thursford, hopefully £1 going to each cause from every book sold.

To my father, George Bolam, an English
gentleman and one of the last.
He died whilst I was planning my adventure
and I hadn't told him what I was hoping to do.
He would have given me a thousand reasons
not to go but, I hope, been secretly proud of
me when I came back.

Chapter 1

1976, GOING NOWHERE

"Kicking around on a piece of ground in your home town
Waiting for someone or something to show you the way
Tired of lying in the sunshine staying home to watch the rain
You are young and life is long and there is time to kill today
And then one day you find ten years have got behind you
No one told you when to run, you missed the starting gun"
Roger Waters, Dark Side of the Moon

No, no, not that kind of virgin. A 53 year old virgin is pretty unusual even in Norfolk. That was all taken care of one exceedingly hot afternoon in the sweltering summer of '76. I was seventeen and Penny, my friend Phil's older sister, was a veritably ancient twenty seven. It all seemed wonderfully exotic to me – not only was Penny blond, attractive and divorced but she had her own flat as well. I felt amazingly grown-up.

For readers of delicate sensibilities, I shall gloss over the gory details. Suffice it to say that it was all over very quickly. Very, very quickly. And if I thought that the relationship would go on all summer and Penny would become my Maggie May, I was sorely disappointed, as I suspect she had been. Whether it was the inadequacy of my adolescent fumblings or the fact that I made a rude and hasty exit to the golf course, I clearly hadn't impressed much and I never managed to get together with Penny again.

A few days later I was presented with the opportunity to lose my virginity all over again. I had picked up a few days work as an extra

5

for a 1930s drama that the BBC were filming around Gloucester-shire and for the princely sum of £17 a day, I suffered the indignity of having my long blond hair cropped in order to hang around the set in a heavy tweed suit for twelve hours at a time in the stifling summer heat, generally doing little or nothing besides getting very hot.

The Production Manager was particularly friendly towards me and even I, as a surprisingly innocent adolescent, could see that that he was pretty camp. However, I knew that he was going out with the production's head make-up girl so I thought that maybe that was just how theatrical people were. Then late one afternoon I called at the wardrobe to pick up my clothes prior to some night filming. My new best friend was there and offered me a lift to the set, which I thought seemed fair enough. On the way he said that he needed to pick up some scripts from his hotel and since we had plenty of time before filming started, we could go up to his room for some tea.

Yes, I know. You can all see what is coming but I am afraid that I couldn't and so I happily, and slightly foolishly, followed on. Ten minutes later room service brought a tea tray up and the conversation for some reason had turned to how fit I was. He leant over and started feeling my biceps, then suddenly and alarmingly made a lunge at me. Thankfully I was strong enough to throw him off and he became almost embarrassingly contrite, telling me that he fancied men as well as girls and begging me not to tell anyone what had happened. Somewhat perplexingly, he also told me that he had thought I would be "up for it" because I had been at a public school, which was an entirely new concept for me. Needless to say, I decided to cut short my fledgling television career.

But I digress, and I'm sorry. You've started reading this to learn about the exploits of a 53 year old on the Arizona Trail and you find yourself wading through the sexual dalliances of a hapless and hopeless 17 year old. I promise you there will be no more of that nonsense – in fact, for several years, there was no more of that nonsense, but that's another story!

Despite the disturbing episode with the man from the BBC, the teenage Jeremy remained pretty pleased with himself, at least for a while. I was heavily tanned after rather too many hours spent lying around in the baking summer sun and very fit after six months of weight training. For the first and last time in my life I was in possession of a six-pack that hadn't been acquired from an off-licence. Better still, the acne that had made most of my teenage years an utter misery seemed to have disappeared almost totally.

Moreover I was back on course after a very mediocre time at school. Somehow I had gone to Cheltenham College as a scholarship pupil and left at just sixteen with little to show for the expensive education that my parents could ill-afford except for two modest A Levels and a posh accent. Clearly the school had not been very impressed either as my headmaster wrote in my final report "It is a pity he is leaving College when he has accomplished so little". I was glad to be out of it.

A year at a technical college known to all around the area as Cheltenham Tech (nowadays grandly titled the University of Gloucestershire) had not only given me a couple of half decent A levels but it had given me back my confidence. Even better, the stutter that had been with me from the age of eight had more or less left me.

I felt ready to take on the world and the particular part of the world that I was set to take on was South Africa. For reasons that I have never fully understood, I had decided that what I wanted to do above all else was to be a mining engineer and work in South African gold mines. Perhaps I had been seduced by the glamorous figure of Richard Hannay, John Buchan's hero in The Thirty Nine Steps, who had been a mining engineer in South Africa. Or maybe I had spent too much time watching the charismatic and brilliant South African Mike Procter play cricket for Gloucestershire, but at seventeen I knew exactly what I wanted to do with the rest of my life. I am not entirely sure that I have had the same certainty at any time in the ensuing 36 years.

With the help of a couple of half-decent A'levels from the afore-mentioned Cheltenham Tech I had secured places to study Mining

Engineering at Imperial College or at Camborne School of Mines together with a scholarship from the Anglo American Corporation to work in South Africa for a year before I went to university.

Now what, I can hear you saying, has all this to do with attempting to walk the Arizona Trail thirty five years later? Well, South Africa was to be the first of half a lifetime of thwarted expeditions. Totally ignoring the fact that not only was I seriously ill-prepared for such an enterprise and that it would quite probably worry my poor parents silly, I wanted to travel to South Africa by bike. My plan was to send some things on ahead and then cycle from Cairo to Cape Town, five thousand miles at 100 miles a day – I should be there in a couple of months. Beyond that I think my planning was utterly non-existent, just exactly what you would expect from a naive and clueless teenager. I really had not thought the whole thing through at all well.

But first I had to get through a fortnight underground at a Cornish tin mine, a prerequisite for Camborne School of Mines. It wasn't exactly what I wanted to do in the middle of the hottest summer Britain had ever had but as things eventually turned out, in an odd sort of way it may have saved me from a disastrous career move. To be honest, I can't remember all that much about it except that I drilled a lot of holes, ate more Cornish pasties in a fortnight than I have eaten in the rest of my life since and wasn't at all bothered by being some considerable distance underground. I think I rather enjoyed myself.

But towards the end of the fortnight my skin started to erupt in an alarming fashion and within days of getting home I was whisked off to the doctor and then to a dermatologist, one of a long line of specialists that had been called upon to examine my troublesome teenage skin from the age of about thirteen. By the time I got to see him, my back, chest and neck looked like a relief map of the Himalayas and was excruciatingly painful.

He took one look at me and did that sucking of the teeth thing that plumbers do when you show them a bit of dodgy pipe work and you just know that they are going to stick another nought on your bill.

"That's the worst I've ever seen", the dermatologist said, a little too enthusiastically for my liking. Later in the consultation he told me that it would probably go by the time I was in my thirties, which was not perhaps the most comforting thing a 17 year old can hear.

The conclusion was that the dust and heat of the mine had brought back my acne with a terrible vengeance and that if I pursued a career in mining, the problem would probably stay with me for most of my life. That autumn I failed my medical with the Anglo American Corporation. The scholarship was off and I reluctantly gave up on the idea of getting a degree in Mining Engineering. There would be no Cairo to Cape Town bike ride. Instead I took a voluntary job coaching tennis and squash at the Starehe Boys Centre in Kenya and headed to Africa by plane instead of by bike. The sun, it was suggested, would be good for my skin. Within weeks I was in Nairobi Hospital, barely able to walk and undergoing tests for, I was later told, Hodgkin's Lymphoma.

Thankfully nobody told me that they were testing my glands for something that in the 1970s I would probably have died from quite quickly and unpleasantly. In any case the tests had apparently proved negative so they decided not to bother keeping me informed about what was going on, which I have generally found is the way with doctors. The best suggestion that the hospital could come up with for my sorry condition was that the acne had become so severe that it was causing my joints to become inflamed as well.

Soon I was back on the plane to England, my African interlude rudely interrupted and a week after landing in England I took a job as a Trainee Insurance Clerk for Eagle Star. So instead of confidently setting forth on a thrilling and life-changing ride to Cape Town I had made a much less thrilling and rather painful journey from mining engineering scholar to trainee insurance clerk in a dreary Gloucester office.

As for the Cairo to Cape Town ride, for years I held on to the hope that one day I might be able to pull it off. I only really gave up on the idea when it became all too obvious that a lone white man with panniers full of money, credit cards, passports and other goodies might find himself popular throughout large swathes of Africa, and not in a good way. Africa had become far too dangerous for solo travel.

Maybe one day.

Chapter 2

MAKING PLANS

"Life is what happens while you are busy making other plans"
John Lennon (after Allen Saunders)

Thirty five years later and Jeremy's big journey had still not left first base. I suppose there was always something else that got in the way. Studying and lack of money whilst I was at university and then straight afterwards I moved to London and jumped on the work treadmill. Six months later I bought my first flat with the largest mortgage I could get hold of and an endowment policy to go with it; then a small house, then a slightly larger house, then a larger one still and then a restaurant. With each one comes a bigger mortgage, another endowment policy, possibly a pension plan and before you know it, if you ever even think of stopping work for more than five minutes, the whole lot will go up in smoke. You are well and truly on a sort of giant human hamster wheel.

Several adventures were planned but none of them came to anything. My bookshelves groaned with Rough Guides to places that I had never been to and probably never will go to and boxes filled up with maps of half the world. Most of my schemes were for elaborate bike rides including Madagascar end to end, America coast to coast and finally, and it was the closest I came to actually setting out, just after the fall of the Iron Curtain I hatched a scheme to cycle through every country in Europe in one go, around fifty countries in all. I still have the big folding map of Europe with my projected route marked on it and a set of Lonely Planet Guides for unlikely places like Russia and the Ukraine.

But somehow I never quite managed to jump off that hamster wheel. There was always another job to be done, a mortgage to be paid and endowment policies to be kept up to date. So I amused myself first with long distance cycling and then long distance running.

My cycling was a bit random but I managed a few tours in France and one across Northern Europe from Holland to Denmark, but at just ten days that didn't quite fit the brief of a really long journey, although my then wife probably thought that it was quite long enough for her liking when I dragged her along with me. Meanwhile I pedalled myself into the ground doing rides all over Britain with an organisation of odd cyclists called Audax, who put on non-stop rides at anything up to 1000k.

Then one day in 1996 I was unexpectedly bitten by the running bug. I was on the wrong end of a particularly good thumping in a squash match at Fulham's extremely smart Hurlingham Club. Simon Eadie was a regular opponent but on this occasion he was clearly far fitter than I would have liked. I asked him how he had got so fit and he told me about a race he had just come back from, 146 miles across the Sahara in six days, carrying all your food and gear for the week. It was called the Marathon des Sables. I decided that it was just the sort of thing I needed to do to keep myself amused and within a week I had sent off an entry form for the following year's race. It would be the first time I had stood on the start line of a running race since the school cross country.

The Marathon des Sables was incredibly tough – heat, dehydration, terrible blisters, you name it, it was all there. I met some great people including Rosie Swayle, who would later run round the world in five years and Chris Moon, who completed the race just a year after getting an arm and a leg blown off by a land mine. It was an unbelievable experience but when I got back to London I was so exhausted that the battered running shoes were thrown in the back of a cupboard, never to be worn again, or so I told everyone.

But soon I couldn't resist another race, then another and another one after that. There was a group of lunatics who would entice each other into increasingly foolish undertakings – someone would ring me up. "Have you heard about this new race? It's called the Trans Siberian 3000 – goes all the way across Siberia in the middle of winter. All the competitors died on it last year. I'm going to do it and so are Mrs Mad and Johnny Bonkers. Are you going to join us?" And if you weren't careful, off you would go again.

I might have failed dismally to get my act together for a really big journey but the ultra distance races were a good substitute. Mostly I would go away to somewhere really interesting for a week or ten days at the most and come back with sore feet and a great tale to tell.

For a while I even had the huge luck to be on Runners' World's list of freelance writers. Steve Seaton, the then Editor of Runners' World would ring me up out of the blue and ask me if I could drop everything and head off to strange races all over the place, run in them and then write a story afterwards. I ran in races as diametrically opposed as the Hull 24 Hour Track Race and the Himalaya 100 Mile Stage Race. I would get free entry to the race, free travel and accommodation and £250 for the article. Happy days!

In the end I raced in Morocco, Mauretania, Jordan, Nepal, India, America, Canada, France, Italy, Switzerland, Iceland, even in Britain, until finally my mind and body decided to say no more and I found I couldn't finish races any longer, however hard I tried and however diligently I might train for them. My right knee was swelling up in protest at nearly forty years of squash and ten years of running every race I came across. Some prodding about inside the aforementioned knee by an expensive surgeon convinced me to give up squash and cut back on running huge distances.

The trouble was that by then I had become a bit addicted to challenges. When you run hundred and two hundred mile races across deserts and over mountains, people who haven't seen you for a while just want to know what your next mad challenge is. Nobody ever asked "How's your family? Or "How is the business going?" All I ever got was "What are you up to next?" I was known as That Crazy Bloke Who Does All Those Stupid Races. It was tough to have to answer their probing with "Nothing much really. I've stopped doing all that stuff," I suppose if I had been given to getting down about things, I might have found it all a bit depressing. I would never be able to run long distances again, I had given up playing squash, which I loved, and I didn't feel old enough take up golf again.

So that pretty much brings you up to date with Jeremy 35 years on from not cycling to South Africa, apart from all the career stuff, which I am sure you don't really want to know about. If you are interested, I've never had more than three days between jobs since leaving university; working briefly and unhappily in The City, first as a commodity broker and then as a life insurance salesman before falling by accident into catering. I managed wine bars in London then set up my own restaurant in Battersea, which I sold after eight hugely enjoyable but exhausting and not particularly profitable years. I moved up to Norfolk to manage a windmill on the North Norfolk Coast and now I look after my own Bed and Breakfast, Holly Lodge in the little village of Thursford. That's all you need to know.

The spring of 2010 found me on holiday in Arizona with Mrs B and her family, who have a small place at the enticingly named Apache Junction on the flat desert country just east of Phoenix. Looming over Apache Junction were the massive rock cliffs of the Superstition Mountains, forty miles long, thirty miles wide and towering more than 4000ft above the Phoenix Valley.

Of course I just had to go up there one day and have a look. In no time at all I was deep into a captivating wilderness of plummeting canyons, soaring rock formations, desert plants and bubbling mountain streams with hardly a soul around to enjoy it apart from me. By midday I had given up on a slightly over ambitious plan to cross the Superstitions in a day and sat down next to a little post with a vaguely triangle shaped symbol on the top. "Arizona Trail" was marked in the middle of the triangle. I examined my map of the Superstitions and found that the Arizona Trail not only crossed the entire mountain range but went off the north and south ends of the map to who knows where. I was intrigued.

The next day I did some research and I think I was probably hooked within minutes of asking Google what it knew about the Arizona Trail. There it was, an almost complete 800 mile trail running north-south right across the entire state, crossing mountains and deserts and dropping down into the Grand Canyon, starting romantically on the Mexican Border and finishing where Arizona gives way to Utah. What a journey that would be. I worked out how far I could walk in a day and how long it would take to do the whole thing. I looked at climate graphs, worked out the best time to go and began to wonder.

Back in England I couldn't quite manage to get the thing out of my head. Months later I was still going back to websites about the Arizona Trail, looking up maps, guidebooks and reports from thru-hikers (the American name for idiots who walk the whole thing in one go). Tentatively I floated the idea with Mrs B, expecting a whole plethora of excellent reasons why I couldn't even consider such a daft idea. To my great surprise, no such objections were forthcoming. Perhaps she imagined that like any number of other big plans, it would all come to nothing in the end. I would buy the books and maps, study them for weeks and then put them in the cupboard alongside the guides to Madagascar, every country in Europe, crossing America, Africa end to end; 35 years of aborted plans all there in a box. Or maybe Mrs B thought it might be a good chance to get some peace for a couple of months. Or permanently if it all went horribly wrong.

I bought myself a copy of *Arizona Trail, the Official Guide*, Tom Lorang Jones' excellent but slightly out of date guide to the trail and studied more and more maps. For my birthday that August appeared a copy of Chris Townsend's account of his thru hike in 2002, *Crossing Arizona*, and I thoroughly enjoyed his detailed descriptions of the trail, impressive knowledge of natural history and his dry wit and occasional political side turnings. By coincidence I had just bought my first copy of TGO magazine, *The Great Outdoors*, and noticed that the same Chris Townsend was their Gear Editor, every month painstakingly comparing ten almost identical pairs of boots, waterproof trousers or hiking shorts and allocating each make a different score.

I was starting to get drawn in by the whole thing and even optimistically mulled over a possible date; spring two years after my first discovery of the trail. That would give me plenty of time to lose interest in the plan, I surmised.

But much to my surprise, and perhaps also that of Mrs B, I didn't lose interest in the Arizona Trail at all and momentum started to gather at an alarming rate. I started swapping e-mails with Chris Townsend, who was very helpful and very encouraging – I don't think that I told him just what a complete novice I was or he might have urged me to go and take a cold shower and think about it more closely. I looked at the notes on gear in the back of *Crossing Arizona* and studied a detailed but disturbingly long list of the kit that Chris had taken on the Pacific Northwest Trail in 2010. Out of around 70 different items on the list, I probably owned about three. I felt fairly confident that I possessed socks, underpants and safety pins but the remaining 67 pieces of specialised hiking gear I would need to research and buy. I didn't even possess a pair of walking boots. What little walking I had done had always been in running shoes.

Bear in mind that although my long distance running might have fooled a lot of people into thinking I was a bit of an outdoors type, and I did like to take myself up a mountain whenever I saw one, which is not often if you live in Norfolk, my sole experience of camping amounted to two brief forays into the great outdoors. I hadn't even been a Boy Scout as a kid.

Aged just fourteen I had donned my widest cord flares and Mott the Hoople tee-shirt and with Stephen Adams, Simon Foster and Tony Stone optimistically set off to walk the Pembrokeshire Coastal Path in just a week whilst camping along the way. We really hadn't quite thought it through properly – the trail is 186 miles long with massive and incessant climbs between beaches and cliff tops. So instead of finishing at a railway station near the end of the path we got about half way round and then phoned my poor father to drive from

Gloucestershire to pick us up, a round trip of at least 300 miles.

Looking back, two things about the trip were of relevance 38 years later. The first was that walking with a pack was substantially harder work than you might imagine so you don't get nearly as far as you think you are going to each day. The second was that I managed to get through the entire week without letting on to my friends that I didn't have a clue how to put a tent up. Somehow I always managed to busy myself elsewhere whilst they were erecting our heavy, old-fashioned canvas tents. Another thing I remember about the trip, of rather less relevance, was that we ate nothing but baked beans all week and yet still happily shared tents with each other.

It was almost thirty years before I ventured forth again into the world of camping, this time for three days on the Cornish Coastal Path with my then girlfriend. Once again, to my great shame, I always managed to find something else to do whilst the tent was going up. And once again I found that covering large tracts of constantly undulating ground with a big pack was harder than I thought, though not as hard as it is when you are fourteen and a bit weedy and your pack is laden down with a canvas tent and a copious supply of baked bean tins.

So there I was planning a solo 800 mile trip into the wilderness with only a vague idea which way up a tent was supposed to go. Pointy bit at the top, I thought. I also had little idea how to make a fire, use a compass, find water, choose a campsite or repair anything that might be damaged. Not only did I not possess any of the required skills needed for the trip but I am probably one of the most pathologically impractical people I know. My DIY skills extend no further than a certain competence at wiping paint onto a wall. If I try to put up shelves or a picture, they will fall down as soon as I turn my back and if I glue anything, it will mysteriously come adrift within minutes. So I found myself perplexed by all the unlikely instruction on Ray Mears' programmes or in The Great Outdoors about building snow shelters, making your own bow and arrows from a piece of hickory or fashioning a pair of snow shoes from birch saplings. All that sort of stuff was light years beyond my limited abilities. I would probably be in big trouble if one of my bootlaces broke.

I should also own up to being a particularly inept traveller. If there is any way of getting myself in a muddle once I leave the safety of my house, I will find it. In the past I have managed to fly to the West Indies and back without my passport, left a rucksack containing my camera and £750 worth of Euros on a French bus, arrived at a Spanish airport exactly a day after my plane home had departed and left my wallet behind on a plane. That is just a small selection of a whole litany of travel mishaps that I have subjected myself and sometimes my unfortunate travelling companions to. I am not safe to be let out of the country alone.

In short, I possessed none of the necessary attributes for the venture beyond a certain dogged determination to finish physical challenges once I start them. The hapless traveller tag I could do nothing about but I set about learning about the intricacies of camping and trekking with great diligence.

I devoured a copy of Chris Townsend's *Backpacker's Handbook*, some of which went straight over my head, but enough sank in to start putting some gear together. If I bought enough kit and told enough people that I was going to do the Arizona Trail, there would be no turning back. I studied everything I could find about the myriad of cutting edge gear available, much of it amazingly light and amazingly clever, though it quickly became clear that the lighter and cleverer stuff was often the most amazingly expensive. My first purchase, though, was a bargain basement second hand tent made by Henry Shires, the Californian tent maker. It cost just £90 and I was thrilled by its minimal weight, but less clear on how to put it up. To my great shame it remained in its stuff sac for nine months until I found a You Tube video on how it worked. I was too embarrassed to "phone a friend".

But soon I was well ensconced in outdoor kit geekdom. No longer was I baffled by baffles. I soon knew all about packability, the fill-power of down, ripstop values, 3-D bionic sphere systems, 6-dimensional elasticity and RodTypePadding. Boot technology I could pick up even more easily. After all, my latest running shoes, and I am not making this up, are currently advertised with Rear and Forefoot Gel, Duomax, SoLyte Midsole, Gender Specific Space

Trusstic, Impact Guidance System, Rearfoot AHAR and Forefoot DuraSponge. Yet I still run like a carthorse.

Soon I was ready for a trip to Britain's Mecca for lightweight back-packers, the Ultralight Outdoor Gear Showroom on Teeside. I took with me a long list of essential kit and Mrs B. It was a great piece of good fortune that I hadn't gone up there on my own. On the way up north I managed to pull off one of my great travel clangers, leaving my jacket including my wallet and credit card hanging on the back of a chair at an A17 farm shop cafe. I am afraid that Mrs B's card took an almighty hammering that day which was later rectified with a large cheque and an expensive dinner out. We returned south with a very satisfactory haul of kit together with my jacket, which was still intact when we phoned the farm shop from a Ripon phone box (Mrs B and I are about the only people in the whole world still refusing to carry a phone).

With six months to go, most of the shiny new kit was still in its wrapping. It was time to unpack it, see if it would all fit in my ruck-sack and head off to the South Downs for a dummy run. A couple of days later, I felt quite chuffed with myself. Not only had I managed to get to Eastbourne by train without going wrong, despite British Rail's best efforts to confuse me by cancelling trains on three different lines, but I had spent a couple of glorious autumn days wild camping on the South Downs Way without major disaster. Aside from an errant fox which spread most of my food and a couple of chewed-up stuff sacs all over the surrounding field, everything went well. Two days in Sussex was a long way from forty in Arizona but it was a start and gave me a little confidence that I might be able to pull this thing off.

I booked tickets to Phoenix for February and even felt bold enough to fix a date to start walking, February 19th, and one when I would stop, March 30th. Readers who have been paying attention may be able to see a pattern emerging of plans that I have not thought through all that well. I would have just 40 days on the trail at around 20 miles every day with no complete rest days. An experienced hiker would have told me to factor in extra days for unforeseen problems and two or three complete days off in the resupply towns. Later I would learn that I had set myself a very tough and slightly foolish schedule.

All the while I carried on researching the Arizona Trail and the things I might encounter along it. Bears and snakes were high up on my list of things I would rather not come across and I am not sure I was greatly comforted by what I found. There had only been ten attacks by black bears in Arizona since 1990 but that sounded like ten too many for my liking. One recent newspaper report told of a man who had "part of his scalp missing" after a bear attack in the Tonto National Forest. I would be walking through there at some stage.

The unfortunate folk of Arizona also suffer around 400 snake attacks each year, making a snake bite a great deal more likely than getting muddled up with a cantankerous black bear. My Audobon Society Field Guide listed, and pictured in vivid Technicolor, some thirty different varieties of snake, only twelve of which are poisonous. The guide suggests that "The victim should avoid moving, as movement helps the venom spread throughout the system, and keep the injured body part motionless." Good advice, I felt sure, but not particularly helpful if, say, a diamond backed rattlesnake took a liking to my ankle in the middle of nowhere. Scorpions and some pretty formidable spiders also looked to be profuse and bothersome in the southern deserts.

My Audobon Field Guide became much thumbed until it would fall open at the bear/ snake/ scorpion pages of its own accord. But I took heart from the news that all of the aforementioned nasties should be hibernating that early in the year. Even so, practically everyone I told about my trek would almost immediately say "What about snakes?" I really don't like snakes.

I tried to get as walking fit as I could, not really believing that you could simply get your "trail legs" on the trail. From everything I read, it was clear that I would probably get stronger once I was underway but I knew that if I wasn't fit enough when I started, I might not last long enough to find out. A staggering 20% of Appalachian Trail thru-hikers drop out within the first week, presumably for physical reasons rather than because they cannot face the dreary prospect of walking through dense forests for more than three months. Even so, it does slightly defy belief that when hikers have planned to walk 2000 miles of a trail, one in five give up only 100 miles into it. So I walked as much as an English winter would allow, trying out my boots and walking with a lightly loaded pack for most of the time. I put in some hard sessions in the gym, often climbing 2,000ft or more on the treadmill with a weighted vest on for extra ballast.

But as I suspected might be the case, the last few weeks turned into a bit of a rush of last minute admin and I probably didn't get in as much walking as I might have hoped for. There were all sorts of bits and pieces to get together, kit to be endlessly sorted and resorted, paperwork and end of year accounts for Holly Lodge, things to arrange for the two months I would be away from the B&B, the Parish Council and my running club, the North Norfolk Beach Runners. I spent a good deal of time gleaning as much information from several extremely helpful Arizonans about the latest trail conditions; water, weather, etc. They all told me I was setting off much too early. Then the local paper and the Eastern Daily Press got wind of my trip and about the charities I would be raising money for and wanted interviews and photo calls, which was all very nice but took up a lot of precious time.

Then to cap it all, just a few days before leaving England, British Telecom kindly arranged for me to have probably the most irritating day of my life. Ever. One morning I decided to check the password on my e-mail account so that I could access and send e-mails from Arizona – it would be the first time for many years that I had bothered to use it from anywhere except my home computer. Despite trying all possible combinations, nothing would work. From my business e-mail address I sent BT one of those "Contact us" e-mails, which in my experience usually gives most companies licence to ignore you, unless you want to buy something from them that is.

To my surprise and then consternation, I got a reply back within a couple of hours. BT told me that my personal e-mail address did not exist. Now bearing in mind that I had been using that selfsame address for thirteen years and that everyone in the entire world who knew me had been using it throughout that time, I found that hard to take. So I phoned BT Broadband to get it sorted out and that is where the nightmare started.

BT Broadband, not surprisingly, had their call centre in India and over the next seven hours, not non-stop I might add as I took a break after four hours for a pee, I spoke at considerable length to nineteen different people. Yes, I did count them, although I may just have spoken to the same half a dozen advisors who just kept passing me around the office. Each one told me that my e-mail address was not in existence, some said that it had never existed and I was given nineteen different, and all very specific, time spans for how long they would need to reinstate it, ranging from 53 days to 17 weeks, none of which was any use to me at all. By early evening I had a distinct, telephone shaped bruise in the middle of my forehead from bashing the receiver against my forehead.

Finally I was left with no option but to start all over again with a brand new e-mail address and send a message to that effect to anyone I could think of. Sadly that was not as easy as it should have been as my computer is the technological equivalent of a teenager's bedroom – stuff is all over the place. Even now, I am still hearing of friends who have sent messages to my old address and think me incredibly rude for not replying.

Just before leaving I got an e-mail from Chris Townsend which he ended with: - "*I wish you good weather, ample water, beautiful camp sites and strong legs.*" Receiving that meant a great deal.

Chapter 3

WORRYING MYSELF SILLY

"The only thing we have to fear is fear itself"
Franklin D Roosevelt

If there was one thing I learned very early on in ten years of long-distance running it was that the longer you have to think about the challenge ahead, the bigger the cold sweat you will be in by the time the starting gun goes off.

I have already touched on how I stumbled by accident into the odd world of long distance running when I entered the Marathon de Sables. More than a thousand experienced runners from all over the world, and also me, flew into Casablanca, then on to Oazazarte for a brief night in a huge luxury hotel before a fleet of trucks came to ship us all out deep into the Moroccan desert to the race start.

It was all immensely exciting and with hardly a moment to breath, there was no time to worry about the task ahead, 146 miles across the Sahara carrying a week's food and gear. Lots of great camaraderie, banter and bravado, genuine for the old hands, somewhat forced for new boys like me.

The problem came when we were dumped in the desert with nearly two days to think about it all and nothing much to do except rearrange our kit again and again, hand in our medical certificates and allow the immensely officious French organisers to check the aforementioned kit in a way that would make the average British tax inspector look like a cockney market trader.

Nothing much to do that is aside from getting in a complete blue funk about the race ahead. I can happily admit that if the organisers had woken us up on the second morning to announce that the race had been called off due to an impending sandstorm in the Sahara, I would have happily packed up my expensive kit, torn up the huge entry fee, set aside 6 months of gruelling training and flown back to England with a glad heart.

Fifteen years on and I can honestly say that I have never really got over that completely irrational fear of running. At local races I have always joined the shuffling queue of shivering runners lining up for the usually limited bathroom facilities on offer.

Before long distance races, I would always spend a mostly sleepless night agonising over the seemingly immense distance ahead, quite clear in my befuddled brain that I just wanted to chuck it all in and head home. However much I tried to tell myself that all I had to do was put one foot in front of the other, then repeat the process again and again until I got to the finish, it was no good, I would always be as nervous as a choir boy singing his first solo.

So I should have known that a two week holiday in an over 55s gated community would give me exactly enough time to get myself into the biggest stew imaginable before setting off on the trail.

Gill's sister and brother-in-law, Wendy and Jim, bought what Americans call a park model and what we would term an unfeasibly large luxury mobile home for little more than the cost of shiny new car in Britain, all furnished and ready to go, with a view to escaping the dreadful Canadian winter to spend some time each year as "snowbirds" in Apache Junction, just outside Phoenix.

Their mobile home (and why are they called that when they never go anywhere?) was of an unimaginable size with three double bedrooms, two bathrooms and a living area bigger than most people have in their houses in England, right in the middle of a one mile square, beautifully manicured trailer park called Superstition Buttes. Buttes, which is pronounced to rhyme with newts, rather than in a snigger inducing manner, are the giant vertical rock formations that so characterise South Western America. Also called mesas, I would come across quite a lot of them in the ensuing weeks.

Life at Superstition Buttes was most seductive with a delightful communal pool to sit by, albeit one that was flooded with country music from dawn till dusk, and warm sunshine to thaw chilled English bones and take away the skin's winter pallor. In the evenings Jim would fire up the barbecue and cook slabs of meat the size of a road atlas and when the air became chilly we would retreat inside where I quickly became a fan of the American version of The Voice and learned all about people like Taylor Swift and Shania Twain by watching The Grammy Awards for 4 hours non-stop.

The Grammys also featured a brilliant performance by the Foo Fighters, an astonishing and slightly bizarre reappearance by the Beach Boys, who looked as if they had all been lifted straight out of Madame Tussauds and a string of awards for Adele. I know that about half the world thinks that Adele is a sort of cross between Dusty Springfield and Kiri Te Kanawa but I just don't get it and never will. She's fine but that's about as far as it goes for me. There, I've just offended 25 million potential readers in one go!

A couple of times we all headed off to one of the many golf courses that have been carved out of the flat, dry as a bone valley that Phoenix sits in. They are quaintly called desert courses but it is hard to imagine yourself in a desert with lush green grass beneath your feet and luxury houses lining every fairway, despite the occasional cactus rearing its prickly head.

However the courses we played were showing signs of losing the battle to grow grass in such an arid landscape. To my consternation it turned out that the Phoenix area was a year or so into one of its driest spells on record. Given that keeping your body topped up with water was one of the Arizona Trail's biggest challenges, that was hardly something to gladden the heart.

I began poring over my trail notes and, sure enough, if the water information was correct, there were vaste stretches where water in a dry year would be somewhere between scarce and non-existent.

I popped into an outdoor shop and bought a couple of extra water bottles but it did occur to me that it didn't matter much how many water bottles I carried, if there was nothing to fill them with, I would still go thirsty.

The water bottles went with the rest of my meticulously acquired kit and as the days went by, I spent more and more time on that favourite activity of anyone with gear, the kit faff. I shuffled things around endlessly to make sure that I had everything I needed; knowing that just one piece of missing kit could mean a hasty retreat back to safety. Little did I imagine that I would manage to lose three essential items even before setting out from Montezuma Pass.

Most days I would peel myself reluctantly away from the poolside to walk into the desert areas a mile or so to the north armed with my Audubon Field Guide to the Southwestern States. Oddly, or perhaps because I was so close to civilisation, I saw almost as many mammals on one afternoon in the scrubland beyond Apache Junction as I would on the whole trail. In a couple of hours I spotted white-tailed deer, jackrabbits and cotton tails, ground squirrels and antelope squirrels and disturbed a large pac of supremely noisy peccaries, also called javelinas, the large pig-like animals that roam around southern Arizona; sadly, the only ones that I would see the entire trip.

However, with just four days to go before setting off for the Mexican Border it felt like a good time to try out a few bits of kit and test my fitness with something more demanding than a flat two hour stroll through Apache Junction's dusty desert scrub. Little did I know that I would get myself into just about as much trouble as it was possible to find in a day's hiking only a few miles outside a major city.

Chapter 4

LESSONS LEARNED BY AN IDIOT ABROAD

"When you find yourself in a hole, stop digging"
Will Rogers, American-Cherokee cowboy and humorist

Just about five miles to the east of Apache Junction looms the massive bulk of the Superstition Mountains. On the west side the Superstitions' seemingly vertical cliffs are split by a gully known as the Siphon Draw, visible from many miles away. For two years I had wanted to climb up the Siphon Draw Trail. I had a photo of the western aspect of the mountains as my desktop and had also been lucky to find on e-bay a small 1930s oil painting by the Californian artist, Helen Newton, showing the same amazing view.

Detailed route notes on the excellent Hiking Arizona website seemed to suggest that even someone with such a poor head for heights as yours truly should be able to climb up the Siphon Draw Trail. From the top I could turn right and walk along the western edge of the range along what is known as The Ridgeline and from there head down to one of the trailheads on the south side of the mountains, thus crossing the Superstions in one glorious, if somewhat tiring day. I thought it would kick start my trail fitness and test out my still fairly new boots on some good, hard Arizona rocks.

Somehow I failed to spot a couple of warnings in the route notes for the Siphon Draw Trail. One said "Be careful – this is the turnaround point for anyone in their right mind" and another warned "There's a section or two requiring you to pull yourself up. Be careful not to go up something you can't get yourself down from".

Now I should declare here and now that for someone who loves mountains, I simply cannot cope when things get a bit vertical. At all. Never have been and never will be able to. Aged 14 in the Combined Cadet Corps at school I scared myself silly on a small cliff face on Cleeve Hill up above Cheltenham and knew then that any serious climbing ambitions had gone out of the window forever. A few years later I dabbled with the idea of joining the army but the thought of some of the rock faces I would have to climb made me shelve the idea.

Still, I set off confidently from the Lost Dutchman State Park just after dawn with a confident stride, a daypack, a bit of lunch, a map and just a couple of litres of water. The last time I had ventured into the Superstions two years before, water had been plentiful in all the mountain streams so I felt pretty comfortable there would be no problem with finding a refill for my bottles.

The clear trail led up to the base of the cliffs until I found myself on the Siphon Draw Trail which soon became steeper. And steeper. And steeper. I passed a few people who were just going up as far as the "turnaround point". Eventually I left them all behind until I was climbing up a path so steep and rocky that I didn't much fancy going back down it. Within sight of the summit, known as the Flatiron, for obvious visual reasons, I reached a section of rock that could only be described as vertical. After several attempts to get up it, getting comprehensively stuck every time, I climbed back down to the bottom of the cliff, sat on a rock, ate most of my lunch even though it was still only 9 o'clock and thought about what to do next. Apart from exactly how I was going to get over the Superstitions that day, things weren't looking too promising for the eight mountain ranges I would have to cross on the Arizona Trail.

Then a near miracle happened, an Irish miracle to be precise. Three climbers suddenly appeared from above, shinning down the cliff as if it was a small ladder. They were Irish lads and to this day I have no idea just what three unequipped climbers were doing up there at that time of the day. I swallowed my wounded pride and told them I had no idea how to get up to the top. One of them shot up the face and back down again, seemingly in seconds. "Like that", he said.

"Er, could you do that a bit more slowly do you think?" I stuttered. He then did exactly what I needed him to do and talked me up the fifteen feet or so of rock, left hand here, right foot there, until in no time at all I was up at the top. He climbed rapidly down again, gathered up his mates, probably said something like "Top of the morning to you" and shot off down the mountain, leaving me shaking my head in disbelief that I had climbed such an edifice.

Fortified by my renewed confidence, the remainder of my lunch and most of my water, I set off for a glorious two hour walk along the ridgeline. The weather was perfect and the views over the Superstition Mountains to my left and the Phoenix Valley to my right 3000ft below were magnificent.

I had read sundry contributions to the Hiking Arizona site suggesting that there was considerable potential for getting things thoroughly wrong on this route but the author of the main article confidently asserted "I do not believe this hike is a route finding nightmare". All I had to do apparently was to walk along the Ridgeline and turn left at the inventively named Peak 5057 where a path marked with a nice dotted line on my map would take me gently down the mountains to the south side of the range where Mrs B was due to meet me at 6 o'clock, shortly before darkness fell.

Now for all sorts of reasons, mostly to do with my own pigheaded-ness but partly down to misreading my newly acquired altimeter watch, I managed to turn left about half a mile before the aforementioned Peak 5057 along what I convinced myself was a path. Fifteen minutes later it became abundantly clear that I had gone the wrong way and that what I had imagined was a path was nothing of the sort and never had been.

That was where I should have turned back and looked for the correct trail. But I happen to have a bit of faulty wiring in my brain which makes me almost pathologically incapable of turning round and retracing my steps. Anyone who has ever gone anywhere with me will know that I can plough on with utter disregard for logic, saying things like "I'm sure there'll be another turning up here somewhere". I always find my way out, eventually, but usually not before

I have irritated the hell out of the people I have led astray.

And so I checked my map and it looked as though all I had to do was cross something called West Boulder Canyon and about a mile of bushwhacking would take me to the Peralta Trail and then on down the mountain. West Boulder Canyon would surely be the valley in front of me, according to the contours on the map. The trouble is it wasn't. Nor was the next valley. Or the one after that.

In short, I put myself through four hours of hell by climbing through no less than six steep sided canyons as the afternoon grew hotter and hotter. The vegetation was dense and spiky, ripping my bare legs to shreds. I did a great deal of sliding down slopes and scrabbling up the other side and reached a number of places so inaccessible that I thought I might be completely stuck.

By now my water had long gone and I was sweating profusely in the dry heat. All of the streams that might have been flowing in the bottom of the canyon were completely dry. I can honestly say that I had never been so dehydrated in my life. My tongue was sticking to the roof of my mouth and my throat felt like sandpaper.

To be fair, I knew that I was heading in the right direction but it was just taking me a very long time to get there and I was getting myself into a seriously exhausted and alarmingly dehydrated mess in the process. Mostly I worried that I hadn't a hope of getting to the trailhead before six o'clock causing everyone to get unnecessarily worried about my wellbeing.

Shortly after 5 o'clock I finally reached the Peralta Trail just near Weaver's Needle, a monolithic and legendary rock formation visible almost throughout the Superstitions. At 6.30 and in total darkness I had descended as far as the Peralta Trailhead, a mile up the track from the appointed meeting place and at least 8 miles from anywhere I might find a taxi. The trailhead was deserted apart from a couple of pick-ups, three or four hairy looking locals and a general sense of packing up after a party.

I approached one of the men, a tall man with a giant ginger beard and long hair to match. He looked like a throw-back to the Beverley Hillbillies. His name was Hugh and after I explained my predicament we agreed that I would walk down to the Carney Springs Trailhead whilst he finished his packing up and if Mrs B had given up on me, he would pick me up and take me on my way.

Quite understandably, Gill was long gone, as was everyone else from such a remote place. Mercifully, Hugh the Hillbilly was as good as his word and not only picked me up but refreshed me with the best tasting Coke I have ever drunk and dropped me right at the gate of Superstition Buttes. It was the first of many small acts of kindness and generosity that I would be offered by Americans in all sorts of places along the trail. My saviour, it turned out, had not been partying with his mates up at the trailhead. In fact he had been doing exactly what he spent most his winter doing; namely taking parties of kids from urban areas of Phoenix up into the Superstitions so that they could learn about their natural environment. "Don't judge a book by its cover," I thought.

Gill, Wendy and Jim had been out looking for me and needless to say, my main meal that evening was humble pie accompanied by a great deal of water. However, I had learned three very valuable lessons which would stay with me over the next few weeks:-

1. Don't think you can climb up and down steep stuff when you clearly can't.
2. If you've lost your way, turn back and start again instead of ploughing on regardless in the mistaken belief that you will find another way through.
3. If you are not sure about water sources, make sure you have plenty with you.

These lessons learned would stop me getting into a lot of trouble in the coming weeks but the day's misadventure had given my fragile confidence a massive knock. Frankly after such a hapless performance in the Superstitions I really doubted if I was competent enough to be let loose on the Arizona Trail without any back up and wondered if for once in my life I had bitten off more than I could chew. But it was too late to back out and I had to somehow get a grip

31

on my fears and give it a go.

Once I had cleaned up my shredded legs and arms and unstuck my tongue from the roof of my mouth, I found one piece of damage from the day's adventure that could not be repaired; the bottom part of one my wonderful Pacer Poles, which I had stuck in my day pack on one of the more precipitous descents, had been pulled away from the top half and probably now lay in the midst of a thorny thicket deep in the mountains. I had just one and a half poles to start the trail with, which is not much use to anyone.

PACER POLES

I had always been a bit sniffy about walking poles, imagining them to be suitable just for very old people, and then only in mountainous terrain. Certainly the sight of walkers on the pancake flat Norfolk Coastal Path armed with two sticks would often make me raise a metaphorical pair of eyebrows. Stubbornly I didn't even change my mind when I saw at least half of my fellow competitors on the incredibly choppy terrain of the Mont Blanc Ultra using them to great effect.

However a pair of increasingly creaky knees had given me cause to do a bit more homework and it seemed that most hard core walkers now use them pretty much all the time. Everything I read suggested that they take a good bit of strain off the legs, allowing you to walk further and faster in a day and with much less pain in any afflicted joints.

Chris Townsend had used a make called Pacer Poles on the Northwest Pacific Trail. Their unique feature is that they have large grips on each pole which fit perfectly into left and right hands whilst most other poles just have a small knob on the top that will eventually feel uncomfortable in your hand.

After a few miles of trying them out in England I was totally old on Pacer Poles and didn't take a step without them all the

---

way along the Arizona Trail. They brought a wonderful rhythm to my stride, took a lot of the strain off my decrepit knees and time after time, they stopped me falling over on awkward terrain. In fact I only fell once the whole trip – a splendid pratfall when the lace cleats on my boots unaccountably got stuck to each other causing me to fall flat on my face in a comedy manner!

Straight away I whistled off an e-mail to Pacer Poles in the Lake District asking them where their nearest distributor was so that I could buy a replacement section. In no time I got a reply from Heather Rhodes in Windermere explaining that they did not in fact have a distributor in the States. However they had e-mailed a friend in Seattle to see if he could send me part of one his poles and they would send a new part to him in due course.

Not long after, I took a call from one Lionel Joyce, a charming man from Seattle who said that he would pack up the bottom section of one of his poles and send it to me by UPS later that day. Sure enough, 36 hours later the poles arrived at the door of Jim and Wendy's park model by UPS courier.

Between them Pacer Poles and Lionel had saved the day and I was able to set off with what would prove to be just about my most crucial piece of kit restored to full health. And neither Pacer Poles nor Lionel would take any payment whatsoever. Superb service from what is clearly a small company that cares a lot about its customers and product and from a complete stranger, the second piece of wonderfully selfless generosity that I had received from an American in two days.

It was now time to leave behind the flesh pots of Apache Junction's Over 55s gated community and head down to the Mexican border, some 250 miles south. Mrs B would have to drive the whole way, our car hire company unaccountably wanting about a month's salary to put a second driver on the rental agreement.

The journey would be something of a sneak preview of just what I would face in the first two weeks of the trail, and yes, it certainly grabbed my attention that a distance we were covering in half a day would take me 14 days to complete on foot on the way back.

On the way we had a look at a couple of towns that I would pass through for resupply, Superior and Oracle. Both looked to have all the luxuries that I needed; somewhere to stay and wash my clothes, a post office, a grocery store and places to eat. But both settlements had a characteristic of American small towns which makes them wholly unsuitable for anyone on foot, namely that they cover a vaste area. Oracle, with a population of less than 2000 was at least 4 miles long and Superior not much more compact. In the next few weeks I would walk many extra miles trudging about looking for all the things I needed in the resupply towns.

The weather on the journey south was distinctly forbidding and as we passed by the great bulk of the Santa Catalina Mountains and the Santa Ritas, the clouds were low and dark and wet looking. At Superior I had picked the encouraging news from a lively lady at the Tourist Information Office who also kept a ranch just outside town, that it had snowed heavily that week. This was all great news for my water worries and might even mean a rare blooming of desert flowers in a week or so. But those mountains did look awfully big.

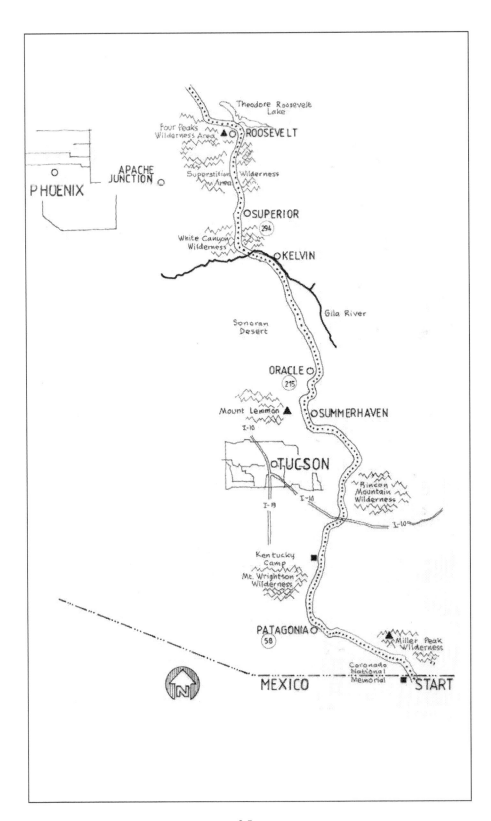

Chapter 5

TENDERFOOT TAKES TO THE TRAIL

MEXICAN BORDER TO PATAGONIA, 54 MILES

"He'd always had a quickening of the heart when he crossed into Arizona and beheld the cactus country. This was as the desert should be with the land unrolled to the farthest distant hills"
Dorothy B Hughes, The Expendable Man

Base Camp to Montezuma Pass

Day 0, February 18th

Base camp for a couple of nights was Ash Canyon, one of the most curious yet delightful B&Bs you could ever encounter, run by Mary Jo Ballator, a lady with attributes that matched those of her B&B. In the middle of nowhere at the base of the Huachuca Mountains some ten miles north of the Mexican Border, Ash Canyon consists of Mary Jo's sizeable straw bale bungalow and one straw bale outbuilding, optimistically called a casita.

Mary Jo was, like many Arizona residents, a refugee from California. She and her husband had moved there some years ago for Arizona's comparatively cheap property values but things hadn't quite worked out and she had been on her own for quite a while. But in a wonderfully Bohemian way she had turned her property into a superb haven for birders, who converge on the Huachuca Mountains from all over the world for its profusion of hummingbirds. Birders and B&B guests clearly gave her some company and I got the feeling that such a charming and intelligent woman would not lack for friends despite the isolation.

Fiercely independent and seemingly caring little for appearances, Mary Jo would emerge from her bungalow covered in parrots and their associated debris to collect $5 a head off anyone who cared to park at Ash Canyon and sit in her garden to see the profusion of hummingbirds that migrate through the area each year. The migration hadn't quite started in earnest, yet in 10 minutes she showed us 15 separate species of bird including nine different, if almost identical, hummingbirds. I was particularly taken with the wonderful light blue Mexican Jays. Sadly in the next few weeks I would struggle to identify one blue jay from another, as indeed I constantly found it difficult and frustrating making anything of what to me were just fast moving dots in the sky or the trees and, believe me, I did try to graduate from the ranks of novice birder. The only birds that I could correctly identify from the beginning of my journey to my last step were ravens, which were all along the trail, in mountains, deserts and forests. Always there and always squawking.

First steps along the trail

The beginning of the Arizona Trail is a curious affair in that it cannot be reached by vehicle so you have to be dropped off at a trailhead called Montezuma Pass, walk the 2 miles to the Mexican border and then irritatingly retrace your steps back to Montezuma Pass from where you head north into the Huachucas. I thought it best to get this slightly false start out of the way so that I could make a quick getaway early the next morning. In any case, it just seemed so wrong to set off on an 800 mile trek with great resolve only to arrive right back at the beginning an hour later. It would also allow me to fiddle about with some photos, take a bit of camcorder footage by the border and stretch my legs after the long journey down.

From the parking area at Montezuma Pass I foolishly set off on the wrong path and arrived back there 10 minutes later, the falsest of false starts. Soon I was on the right trail on a lovely sunny, cool afternoon with the great yellow plains and mountains of Mexico stretching out in a golden haze to the south.

The border itself was a huge anticlimax. Perhaps I had expected a massive grey wall topped with machine gun toting US troops but one moment I was walking down a gentle hillside at 6000ft, high above the Mexican plains below and then suddenly there was the border, a scrappy little broken barbed wire fence and a small monument simply marked "102". After looking furtively around I stepped over the fence and back just so I could say I had been to Mexico, half expecting a dozen border guards to emerge noisily from the scrub and arrest me for illegal entry into America.

Arizona seemed to have a strange attitude towards Mexico. At Apache Junction I had met a number of people who were happy to voice a very low opinion of Mexicans and several times when I told people where the trail started from, they would say something like "You don't want to go down to the border – there are Mexicans down there". Well of course there are, that's why they call it Mexico!

And yet just as we in Britain need Eastern Europeans to do all the dirty, cold and unpleasant jobs that British people don't want to do any more, I am not sure quite how the southern states of America imagine they would get their dishes washed, their pools cleaned,

Mexican border

their roads mended and their fruit picked without the Mexicans and other Hispanics who do all those jobs.

Whilst the vast majority of people I met on my journey were very fair minded and often quite liberal in their ideas, Arizona also has a highly vocal red-necked tendency with an apparent dislike for Mexicans, Hispanics, Coloureds, Chinese, Pinko Liberals, Environmentalists, Evolutionists, Pacifists and the Anti-gun Lobby. Since I probably qualified for membership of at least four of those groups I thought it best to keep my mouth shut concerning political issues whilst out on the trail.

Meanwhile I took a few photos at the border and mulled over the conundrum of 140 million people who could legally work on one side of that little fence and 70 million on the other side who would like to.

Day 1, February 19th.

Montezuma Pass to Parker Canyon, 23 miles

My last evening before hitting the trail was spent thrashing around the nearby town of Sierra Vista in an ultimately successful attempt to replace my newly acquired Gorilla Pod (a small, bendy camera tripod which attaches to rocks and trees), left behind somewhere near the border fence and without which I would not be able to take photos or camcorder footage of myself. Later that evening I also managed to lose a US/British adaptor plug vital for charging my Kindle, my camera or my camcorder. After e-mailing Mrs B from Patagonia to send me another from Norfolk, I found it two weeks later neatly tucked into my waterproof top. But after the Pacer Pole episode and now this, I reasoned that at the rate I was going I would have an empty pack by the time I got half way to Utah. In fact after the gorilla pod, the Pacer Pole and the adaptor plug I didn't lose another piece of kit on the whole of the trip.

Everyone I met in the border area seemed only too keen to warn me about the presence of "illegals" (Mexicans and drug-runners) in the Huachuca Mountains. But I reckoned that if you were trying to smuggle either yourself or drugs into America, you wouldn't be bothering a lone hiker camping in the wilderness. Even so the warnings were stark from the Border Control Police and in the Arizona Trail notes too and I didn't want to worry those following my progress that my first day on the trail might be my last. There was also a fair amount of snow higher up the mountains.

So I decided to give everyone, including myself, some peace of mind and take the low route recommended for mountain bikes which wound through the foothills of the Miller Peak Wilderness. As it turned out, it was a good decision. Unsurprisingly I didn't see any illegals but there was a stiff, cold westerly blowing right across the mountains and dark snow clouds on the top of the peaks. Gill took me back up to Montezuma Pass just after dawn and with no great ceremony we said our goodbyes and I set off up the track that led inexorably north for more than 800 miles.

My first day on the trail proved to be one of the easiest I would have for many weeks; a red dust track wide enough to take a vehicle with some ease, gently hugging the contours of the lower slopes of the Huachuca Mountains to my right, the land dropping away to the parched plains of Northern Mexico on my left. Apart from a few white-tailed deer and the lovely bright blue Mexican Jays swooping through the scrublands, the only signs of life anywhere were several white and green Border Patrol 4x4s patrolling the area with great diligence.

It occurred to me that the much trumpeted illegals would stand little chance of getting through this area. The Border Patrol vehicles were numerous and several slowed down as they passed me to take a closer look – one or two of the vehicles were even equipped with some sort of radar or satellite on their roofs.

By two o'clock my fresh legs had taken me to Parker Lake, a man-made lake of some size and the only one for 200 miles in any direction. I had thought of camping by the lake for my first night but I was going well and it was much too early to stop, although the thought of a couple of hours lying on the shore in the afternoon sun was most seductive.

Besides, the official campground was already filling up for the President's Day Holiday with massive RVs, the recreational vehicles favoured by Americans keen to transport nearly all of the contents of their house with them when they go travelling. I figured that the most recreation the RVs' occupants would be getting that weekend would be when they made a big barbecue.

I wondered what Americans felt about President's Day. Election fever was, if not exactly gripping the country, at least taking quite a hold in the media and although Obama's popularity rating was far from good, he looked like a reincarnation of John F Kennedy in comparison to the bizarre collection of dangerous maniacs, accident-prone buffoons and crashing bores climbing over each other to get on the Republican ticket. I supposed that whatever the country thought of its President, at least it was a free day off work.

So I bathed my by now rather hot and overstressed feet in the lake, filled up with water and after a couple of false starts, found the trail heading away from Parker Lake westwards. A mile or two on I stepped aside for a small party of people on horseback, the only one I would see all along the Arizona Trail, although it is apparently used quite a lot by people wanting to play at being cowboys for a few days.

By 5.30 I had found a lovely place to camp, flat and sheltered and nestling by the babbling brook of Parker Canyon. To my great delight I managed to put up my Henry Shires Tarptent without it collapsing in a heap, made a little fire of twigs in the Ti-Tri Inferno stove and settled down for the night feeling quite pleased with myself.

ARIZONA GEOGRAPHY

The Arizona Trail runs pretty much due North for 800 miles from the Mexican Border as far as Utah, carefully skirting the big cities of Tucson and Phoenix and instead sticking as far as possible to Arizona's wilderness areas. It was conceived by Dale Shewater around 30 years ago and since then the Arizona Trail Association has organised an enthusiastic band of volunteers to produce a complete trail. The last mile was finished about two months before I set out and if I could get to Utah, I would be the first person to walk the completed trail.

The state is split into northern and southern halves by the Mogollon Rim, a huge escarpment hundreds of miles long that marks the southern edge of the Colorado Plateau. To the south are hot, arid desert lowlands which from a distance can look quite flat but are much bumpier than they look. Out of the desert, which is mostly about 4000ft above sea level, rise numerous isolated but high mountain ranges known as sky islands. Many of them climb to well over 10,000ft and the Arizona Trail crosses eight of them. The net result is that you can see for vast distances and can often identify a mountain range up to 100 miles away. It makes navigation easy but can be a little daunting when you look at what lies ahead of you.

To the north, the Colorado Plateau is much flatter, much wetter and has far more trees than the south and none of the cacti and desert plants that characterise the southern deserts. Most of it lies at around 8000ft and the only part of the northern end of the trail which is not largely flat is the plunge in and out of the Grand Canyon, which drops down to 2000ft and then climbs steeply up to the even higher Kaibab Plateau running all the way to Utah.

Those wanting to complete the trail in the spring always start in the south in the hope that by the time they reach the Colorado Plateau, the winter will have passed. I had been warned by several people in Arizona that I was starting much too early and so would probably see a lot of snow in the north but I was stubbornly determined to get back to England before my Norfolk Bed and Breakfast started to get busy, which meant getting home by Easter.

Day 2, Parker Canyon to Red Rock Canyon, 18 miles

Whilst my first day on the trail had done everything it could to build up my fragile confidence, the second day did a great job of knocking it back again. That, I would find in the ensuing weeks, was to be a typical pattern. Good days and bad, highs and lows, confidence restored one moment and then the next, huge doubts about how much further along the trail I could go.

My first night in the wilderness was a bit of a shock. It was way colder than I had expected so far south. I shivered my way through the small hours, putting on more and more clothes and at 6 o'clock my watch read just 26F and there was frost on the inside of the tent. Packing up to get on the trail took until half past eight. I was too cold to get moving properly and even with gloves on, my numb fingers felt like frozen sausages and refused to work well enough to fill up my stuff sacs.

I was keen to press on and get within striking distance of the little town of Patagonia where I had booked somewhere to stay for the next night, confident that I could reach there in three days. The terrain looked easy heading northwest across the innocuous looking Canelo Hills, low yellow hills of dry grass, oaks, juniper and ponderosa pine brightened everywhere by the spectacular shrubs called Mexican Manzanita, all rusty red bark and bright pink blooms, the only flowers to be seen anywhere.

But what looked easy on the map, and walking invariably looks easy on a map, proved to be anything but as the trail switch backed up and down the Canelo Hills with monotonous regularity. I must have made a dozen 500ft climbs in the day as the morning cool gave way to a hot and dusty afternoon. My feet were showing tell-tale signs of "hot spots", that angry feeling familiar to every walker or runner which means that blisters are just waiting to pounce and get you.

By six o'clock I had had enough and made camp near the obviously named Red Rock Canyon, perhaps a little too close to ranch cattle for comfort but I found a place not far past a water tank where the ground was relatively free of dung. It was to be another very

Green energy old and new, Red Rock Canyon

unpleasant and cold night with the temperature falling to an alarming 19F despite the trail having dropped down 1000ft from Parker Lake. I wore every single item of clothing in my bag, including gloves and beanie, and felt slightly more comfortable.

Just after midnight I woke to a fearful howling not far from my tent. The noise came from all around and went on for at least ten minutes – it was probably just coyotes, which are inclined to howl in a disturbingly eerie manner but my diary note that it was "quite unsettling" may have been the understatement of the year.

I slept fitfully after that and found myself wide awake at 4 o'clock with a head full of dark, gloomy and negative thoughts. What on earth was I doing all this for? With sore feet, cold and exhausted after just two days of relatively easy terrain I could see no chance of finishing such a mountainous trail or even of getting half way. I thought seriously of packing it all in at Patagonia and heading home on the next plane.

40 DAYS AND NIGHTS IN THE WILDERNESS

For reasons largely beyond my comprehension I was on a self-imposed schedule of getting to Utah in less than 40 days. It is fair to say that I am not the world's most regular churchgoer but I had somehow latched on to the hair-brained idea of 40 days and nights in the wilderness to coincide, more or less, with Lent. Plus I like to make things difficult for myself.

To that end, I had booked in advance return flights from Page to Las Vegas and onward to London, which gave me a bare 40 days on the trail and a day to get to Page. I would need to average 20 miles a day, which is quite a lot with a full pack. If anything went wrong such as bad weather or illness or if I took a day off to rest, the target average would creep up rapidly in the manner of England's cricket team chasing an unlikely one-day target.

It was a tough call, and probably somewhat foolish and led to me doing more miles on many days than was entirely comfortable. At the end of each day I would try to "go the extra mile" and instead of stopping when I was tired or had found somewhere nice to camp, I would plough on for an extra mile or so to get as far up the trail as I could.

Day 3, Red Rock Canyon to Patagonia, 11 miles

The eleven mile stretch into Patagonia would be one of my easiest days of all – a few more miles of what the trail notes described as "quite a bit of up and down" then a ramrod straight three miles up the tarmac of the Harshaw Road through the homesteads surrounding Patagonia. As well as correctly describing the up and down, the trail notes also suggested that I might "catch a glimpse of the rare violet-crowned hummingbird or northern beardless-tyrannulet". Needless to say, I didn't.

However what I did see just about a mile on from my camp was a dead cow right by the side of the trail, not a pleasant sight and very,

very smelly. I pictured Liam Neeson in "Rob Roy" hiding in the carcass of a highland cow to escape the dastardly English Redcoats and thought it unlikely the soldiers would have failed to hear the sound of Rob Roy vomiting prodigiously .

A little further on I ran into a uniformed Border Control Guard complete with a very large sub-machine gun. He and a helicopter hovering overhead were apparently looking into an alleged sighting of an illegal in the area. He asked me if I had seen anyone and I told him no, but I had seen a dead cow. Somehow he didn't seem much interested in the cow but could not have been more charming, if a little intimidating.

Just outside Patagonia I saw the policeman again, this time in his vehicle. I asked him if they had found anyone and he said they hadn't seen a soul, adding without a trace of irritation that I might have been the suspected illegal they were looking for. I didn't feel too bad if I had wasted their time – I think he was just glad to be out in the fresh air for a few hours.

I got into Patagonia at midday, so early in fact that I disturbed Kayti getting my room ready at her impressively named Sheffield Manor, my home for the night. Sheffield Manor was much more modest than its name suggested, my room being furnished in a strange, dark, dark style and including no less than three air conditioning units and a complete range of home made kitchen and bathroom units. Still, it was clean and comfortable and all I needed. But instead of hovering around in an irritating fashion waiting for Kayti to finish, I trotted off to collect my post box and find some much needed lunch.

POST BOX

To lighten the load in my pack I used a post box system which involves filling a cardboard box with all the things you might need on the trail but don't want to carry in your pack and posting it on to yourself marked "for collection by thru-hiker". Then when you reach the next town it is there waiting for you. You hope.

Mine contained stuff like clean clothing to wear in town, a supply of lithium batteries, chargers for Kindle, camcorder and camera, a couple of reference books, a stack of large envelopes each containing the notes and maps for the next section of the trail and a copious supply of things to treat my feet with. Altogether it weighed about 10lbs, around half the weight of my pack without food and water so it saved me carrying a lot of unnecessary poundage.

The much maligned US Postal Service worked brilliantly and in each town a cheery Post Office was ready to hand me my package. The only time I had to do without my extra gear was at Superior, which I had worked out I would probably reach on a Saturday afternoon, and did. So with the Post Office not opening until Monday morning I sent it straight on to the next town nearly a week away at Pine.

Each little Post Office was clean and efficient and always a hub of the local community. I would often stand there in the queue for a while listening to snippets of conversation from the postmistress such as "Hi Marge. How's Jack doing after they did his prostate?" "Fantastic. He says it's 20 years since he's had such a good pee". Clearly life in small town America was not much different to that in North Norfolk.

Patagonia was a delightful little town, its wide main street lined with mostly old, brightly painted two storey buildings and happily for someone coming off the trail containing such unaccustomed delights as cafes and delis. Outside one eatery, I spotted a fit looking man clad in specialist walking gear and poring over a collection of maps. I couldn't resist checking him out and he turned out to be the only fellow Arizona Trail hiker I would come across for many weeks. Mike Elliot was an ex mining engineer from Tucson and he was doing the trail in lengthy sections. I had spotted his large boot prints in the trail dust for a couple of days. His plan was to hook up with a friend the next morning for a day on the trail and then continue on his own as far as Tucson, break for a family wedding and do the remainder sometime later in the spring.

That evening I ran into Mike and his charming wife, Judy, at Patagonia's only pub, The Wagon Wheel. We made a tentative arrangement to walk together the next day and then I left them to it, partly because I felt they might want some time together if Mike was going to be on the trail for two weeks and partly because the excellent beers I had skulled a little too rapidly meant that I wasn't all that sure that I was still making much sense.

I never saw Mike again. He was a bit slow off the mark in the morning and I was well on my way by the time he got going. But some time after I got back to England I had a worrying e-mail from Judy – Mike had gone missing further up the Arizona Trail and she wanted to know what to do about it and what that part of the trail was like. The section he had disappeared on I knew to be tricky and precipitous with ample opportunities to lose your footing and tumble some distance in a messy fashion, but I kept that information to myself and told Judy that I was sure he would turn up soon. Thankfully he reappeared a day later and the story was no more dramatic than a flat battery on his cell phone or being out of range of a signal.

Clearly though, Mike did not lose all his brownie points with that episode as he is now planning to hike the much longer Pacific Crest Trail, something that he had been wanting to do since his early twenties but just never quite got around to. I felt that our back stories had a great deal in common.

Early the next morning I left Patagonia with a heavy heart. Everyone had been so charming; I felt I could have stayed there for days and chat to the incredibly helpful volunteers at the library or to Ann Caston, an elderly lady who kept the tourist information office open for an extra hour just so that I could send an e-mail to Mrs D to ask her to mail an extra fitting for my camcorder charger and a supply of Compeed for my feet. Ann and I talked for ages about all sorts of things, mostly politics and it was only the lure of The Wagon Wheel's beer that made me leave her delightful company.

CHAPTER 6

INTO THE CACTUS COUNTRY

PATAGONIA TO ORACLE, 145 MILES

"Most of my wandering in the desert I've done alone, not so much from choice as from necessity. I generally prefer to go into places where no one else wants to go. I find that in contemplating the natural world my pleasure is greater if there are not too many others contemplating it with me at the same time"
Edward Abbey, Desert Solitaire

Day 4, Patagonia to Tunnel Head, 20 miles

I suspect most Arizona Trail thru-hikers feel that they are only properly underway when they leave Patagonia, although from the disappointing condition of my feet and the generally battered state of my body when I arrived in the town, I am not sure that I quite saw the first 55 miles as simply a short overture to warm up the orchestra.

Even so, I had only been on the trail for 2½ days and since my general direction of travel had thus far been West-North-West, I was still just a paltry 15 miles from the Mexican Border. When I had studied the complete map of the Arizona Trail in Ann Caston's little Tourist Information Office and saw how far I had come, the remaining 750 miles looked like a very, very long way indeed.

My next port of call would be Oracle, 145 miles and 3 mountain ranges away, one of the biggest stretches between resupply towns on the entire trail. It would be at least a week before I would see more food, a laundry and a comfortable bed so I left the delights of Patagonia with a very full pack indeed. Mike Elliot was nowhere to be seen as I checked in my box at the Post Office at 8 o'clock and headed up the dirt road leading north out of town.

For 13 miles the increasingly rocky track led more or less straight up hill into the Santa Rita Mountains. Although I only saw one other person all morning, a dog walker just outside town, the track was wide enough to take a 4x4, not one for the walking purist perhaps but it was great to be able to just amble along without studying where my feet were going all the time.

The day quickly became very hot, as always seems to be the case when you are walking uphill, and I was pleased not to be climbing the pyramid peak of Mount Wrightson to my left, snow-capped and a further 3000ft up. Instead the Arizona Trail obligingly crossed a saddle at a mere 6600ft, 2500ft above Patagonia. At the top I left a note for Mike Elliot, who was nowhere to be seen, wishing him all the best for the rest of the trail.

Water was plentiful once I passed the saddle and with my food heavy pack I was grateful not to need to carry too much extra ballast, although the going did become mercifully cooler as the path dropped down through a dense oak and pine forest to the old mining area around Tunnel Head. If you looked closely through the undergrowth you could still see signs of the ambitious mine workings constructed by the Santa Rita Water and Mining Company in the early 1900s.

Gold had been discovered on the east slopes of the Santa Ritas in 1874, the biggest deposits in Southern Arizona, but this was "placer gold" which needed copious quantities of water to entice it out of the sand and gravel. Water was seasonal and scarce and carrying water up and down the mountain made extracting anything worthwhile monumentally hard work. Mining stopped in 1886 and it was only when James Stetson, a mining engineer from California came up with an unlikely plan to build a two mile long aqueduct to fill a specially constructed reservoir with the spring snowmelt that it started again.

Sadly Stetson died shortly after the aqueduct was completed, killed in a mysterious fall from a Tucson hotel balcony in 1905 and his wealthy backer, George McAnemy lost most of his money in a messy divorce soon afterwards. The operation folded and little gold was ever extracted, a sad result for the massive effort needed to build an aqueduct to take water two miles uphill in such a remote area. Now the area has largely reverted to a pristine wilderness, which is probably a good thing.

I made camp early near a lovely bubbling stream close to Tunnel Head and gloomily examined my feet, which were starting to go through in a number of places. This was not good news – in the past bad blisters had forced me out of long distance races in the diametrically opposed locations of Hull and Death Valley so I was keeping my fingers crossed that some strategically placed Compeed might see me through until my feet got used to the unaccustomed punishment they were being subjected to.

If only more of the trail had been this good

Day 5, Tunnel Head to beyond Oak Tree Canyon, 18 miles

If much of my first four days on the trail had been a largely solitary experience, coming down from the Santa Ritas I ran into a bewildering number of people, probably because the area was within striking distance of Tucson.

Not far down the trail I was hailed by a hiker at the Garden Canyon Road Trailhead, "Hi, you must be Jeremy. Mike told me all about you". It was Mike Elliot's friend, Chris, and he was heading back up into the Santa Ritas to meet Mike who was apparently at least 5 miles behind me.

Four miles on and I reached Kentucky Camp where I had high hopes of a splendid breakfast. Kentucky Camp was built in 1904 as the headquarters of the doomed Santa Rita Mining Company. Today it is maintained as a historic building, which in Arizona is pretty much anything over 20 years old, and people can stay there apparently. But although there were hordes of day hikers hanging around, there was a disappointing absence of refreshments to be found anywhere in the place. I wandered gloomily from empty room to empty room but drew a complete blank.

I mused that if we had such a building in England, we would hand it over to the National Trust who would fill it with period furnishings, put in a tea room and a shop selling knick-knacks and charge you a small fortune to get in. I wasn't sure which was the more authentic but I know that at that moment, the tea shop option would have got my vote every time.

Before leaving Kentucky Camp I sought out the Forest Ranger and found him relaxing in the morning sun outside his mobile home. He was very elderly and somewhat deaf. I filled up one of my water bottles from his hosepipe which dispensed warm, rubber flavoured water and he reassured me that I needn't worry about water, I would find a stock tank every two or three miles. In fact the first water I found was 7 miles away and the next 10 miles after that. I spent much of the day extremely thirsty and decided that I wouldn't be adding that particular Forest Ranger to my next Christmas card list.

The maze of tracks leading away from Kentucky Camp was surprisingly busy and I was profoundly irritated by several buffoons on fast, noisy quad bikes. Better company were two good old southern boys in a pickup who kept leapfrogging me as I plodded up the dusty track. They were out panning for gold as a hobby and one showed me a tiny phial containing minute specks of gold. When he heard I was British he surprised me by saying "Aar served with yous boys in the Sinai" and when we finally parted he bade me farewell with a phrase that I believe not to be native to Arizona, "Pip, pip and all that"!

Medical issues and lack of water filled my thoughts as I negotiated the small hills north of Kentucky Camp. Not for the last time on the trail, I found myself troubled by a slightly too active digestive system and my feet were starting to give me real cause for concern. My left foot was in poor shape and the Compeed I was using had come away from my hot and sweaty skin to form lumps that were rubbing yet more blisters. I became worried about getting infected feet as my socks got dirtier and dirtier on the long trail to Oracle. I know that I must have been somewhat self-absorbed as I have absolutely no recollection of just where I camped that night.

WATER SOURCES

With dire news in the local media about Phoenix's driest winter on record I found myself much preoccupied in the early days on the trail with thoughts about water and exactly where I might find it. The Arizona Trail notes were very specific and hugely helpful. Without them, with the best will in the world, you are not going to find a spring that is 200 yards away from the track and deep in the forest if you don't know it is there. But even with the help of the trail notes I didn't always manage to locate the water sources described, which could be frustrating if you had walked a mile off the trail to fill up your bottles. Sometimes a water source would be dry when you found it. All deeply irritating if you are thirsty and the next water on your map is three hours away.

But most of the time I found water pretty much where it was supposed to be. I took it from mountain streams and springs, from cattle tanks and troughs, from ponds and lakes, from muddy puddles and one day, as a last resort, by filling my bottles with snow and hoping it would melt (which it didn't). The water from mountain streams was clear and lovely and I seldom bothered to treat it with anything but a lot of the water sources were distinctly murky with all sorts of things that I didn't much want to think about floating inside.

I carried with me a brilliant device called a Steripen, which is about the size of a chunky pen. When you press a button on the side of it and immerse it in your water bottle and stir for about 90 seconds, the Steripen emits an ultra violet beam which sterilises the water and it is ready for drinking straight away. I also carried a supply of tiny Oasis water purification tablets to use as an extra something if the water looked really filthy.

The fact that I never once upset my system with dodgy water must mean that the Steripen worked. I did get thirsty a few times but never disastrously so. Sometimes I was probably not carrying quite as much water as I should have been but I always believed that I would find some more soon, and mostly I did.

Day 6, Oak Tree Canyon to Cienaga Creek, 24 miles

I really needed to crack on today. I wanted to make it all the way to Cienaga Creek, 22 miles away, leaving me with another 20 miles to get up to Grass Shack Camp, high up on the Rincon Mountains where the Saguaro National Park regulations had required me to book a camp ground in advance, a difficult rule for thru-hikers as you probably won't know a week ahead just which day you will get there.

But the terrain was easy, the winding path dropping down pleasantly towards the base of the Rincons. For much of the day I crossed gently undulating open grasslands. By now Mount Wrightson and the Santa

Ritas were receding into the distance and the great bulk of the Rincons loomed large to the north. In fact it looked so big that it was hard to believe that the top of the range was still two days away.

This was a new section of trail and I couldn't help wondering if it had been designed more for mountain bikers on a day out from Tucson than for walkers. Again and again I found myself heading back south as the trail contoured around the low hills – mountain bikers don't much mind their paths winding all over the place whilst walkers prefer to take the most direct route possible. That must have been a dilemma for the trail builders and I am not entirely sure they got the balance quite right. At any rate, I saw lots of mountain bikers gleefully hammering along the track whilst I appeared to be the only person out there happy to spend a hot day walking round in little loops.

I was firmly in cactus country now. There were forests of prickly pear, massive barrel cacti and chollas, many with brilliant yellow fruit and the characteristic multi armed Saguaro which pretty much only grows within 200 miles of Phoenix and whose flower is the Arizona State Flower (if you ever see a saguaro cactus in a film, it will have been filmed in Arizona, not wherever else it is supposed to be set). Fortunately they were all far enough away from the trail not to be a nuisance but later that week I would have several comedy encounters with cacti, much to my discomfort.

Late in the afternoon as I crossed under the busy Interstate 10 Highway which runs from Tucson to El Paso, I felt as though I had come out the wilderness and was right back in what we call civilization. The haze of Tucson was just visible 20 miles to the North West, the occasional plane flew overhead from Tucson Airport and I now found myself sandwiched between the I-10 and the busy railway line that carries mile long freight trains east-west across the country.

But a mile or so further on I came upon the wonderful quiet oasis of Cienaga Creek where tranquil blue green waters were surrounded by cottonwoods in their bright green spring cloak. I took my pack off and determined that this might just be the loveliest place I would camp at on the entire trail, just the job for soothing my troubled feet

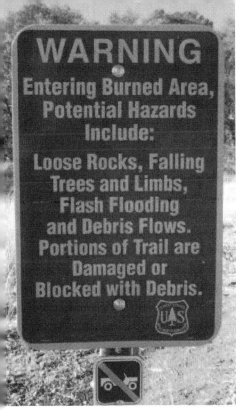

▲ *Thankfully I never saw any "falling limbs"*

▲ *Barrel Cactus*
▼ *Cienaga Creek*

and well out of earshot of the I-10 and the railway. Minutes later a man came by with his son – he warned me that at night mountain lions, racoons and javelinas come down to the creek to drink, "sometimes bear too", he added, a little too theatrically.

I pondered this advice and wondered if this was something he had made up to entice his son away from his TV and games console for a walk down to the creek to see all sorts of exciting and possibly dangerous animals. However I knew that once night fell I would be spooked by every rustle of the cottonwoods above and would very probably not sleep a great deal for contemplating the prospect of sharing my tent with a mountain lion or two.

Reluctantly I picked up my pack and moved on, crossing the railway line and moving on into the dusk to camp as far away from the trains as possible.

My night under the Rincon Mountains would be my most disturbed on the whole trail even though I had camped carefully in a sheltered hollow fully a mile beyond the tracks. Every ten minutes all night long a mile long freight train would approach, its rumble building up like a jet getting ready to take off and every few seconds the hooters would blow. "Why oh why do they have to blow their bloody hooters all the time", I wondered bitterly as the umpteenth train thundered by. Do they give the loudest hooters to the most senior drivers or do they hand them out to the ones with the smallest dicks just to cheer them up, like Porsches to bankers? The romance of Jack Kerouac jumping freight in On the Road or Edward Abbey doing the same at Flagstaff somehow passed me by at that moment.

Day 7, Cienaga Creek to Grass Shack Camp, 18 miles

My first day in the Rincons was a day of great contrasts. After the disturbed night, the long approach to the base of the Rincons went on forever across the Saguaro punctuated grasslands. Weary and hot, I felt quite dispirited, particularly when both Colossal Cave and Hope Camp turned out to be somewhat disappointing. Despite the

▲ *Approaching the Rincons through a saguaro forest*

▼ *Pop C*

trail notes giving me no expectation of any refreshments at either, I still harboured hopes that one or the other might supply me with at least a cup of coffee. Earlier the dude ranch at La Posta Quemada had been closed and I had to content myself with another bowl of porridge for breakfast together with some water from the washrooms at the La Selvilla picnic area. Still, splashing my face and washing my battered feet in running water was a real treat.

But as the track began its steep climb up from the Hope Camp at 3000ft my mood began to lift. The path up the mountain was a marvel of trail building, huge slabs of stone creating giant staircases that climbed up and up the mountainside. It looked to have been made quite recently and I wondered how they had done it and admired those who must have given up many weekends so that I, and apparently nobody else could climb the Rincons with ease.

I say apparently nobody else as at that moment I was shaken from my reverie by a booming voice from above shouting "Jeremy". I looked up and clambering down the steep slope was a big bear of a man with a profuse grey beard, a medium sized backpack and a bright yellow hiking shirt. He introduced himself simply as Pop C, the trail steward for the Rincon Mountains section. He had been following my progress on SPOT and had come out to offer support and more importantly, food.

We sat down in a shady spot out of the fierce afternoon sun and chatted about the trail for half an hour, sharing oranges of unbelievable succulence. As we parted, he handed me a small bag of food for my evening meal; chicken, rice and broccoli with a Clif Bar to follow, veritable riches after the diet of noodles I had supped on for the past few days. I reflected on the unrestrained generosity of Americans and wondered how many British people would drive 30 miles out of their city and climb 2,000ft up a mountain in search of a total stranger, just to offer him their support.

Pop C's appearance cheered me greatly and after washing my feet and replenishing my water supply in a magnificent, wide, fast flowing mountain stream, I cracked on to Grass Shack Camp, half way up the Rincons. Deep in the oak and pine forest at 5300ft it was a

WHAT IS A SPOT?

Before setting out I mulled over how best to keep myself reasonably safe and how to avoid people back home worrying too much about my wellbeing. Mobile phones would be out of range on most of the Arizona Trail and satellite phones are extremely expensive to buy and not much cheaper to rent, even for just a couple of months. I opted for a neat little device called a SPOT, so simple a gadget that even I could manage to operate it successfully.

Bright orange and about the size of pack of 25 cigarettes, SPOT is a satellite tracking system. Once you have registered your device, and even that allegedly simple process almost defeated me, you can register your position as often as you want. Each evening the first thing I would do before making camp would be to activate the SPOT and anyone looking up my position on a computer map would know exactly where I was to within a few yards. There was a second button which thankfully I never had to use which calls emergency services to your rescue in the event of serious injury or illness. Clearly not to be used just because you have run out of loo paper or coffee, it was a great comfort to know that I could get pulled out if I got into big trouble. There were times on the trail when I didn't see another living soul for three days and would probably not have made it out if I had fallen and broken a leg. Aaron Ralston would have saved himself a great deal of anguish and all that messy business with a penknife if he had taken a SPOT into that Utah canyon but, my goodness, the world would have missed a great story.

I think that lots of people back home enjoyed following my progress but I sometimes had mixed feelings about being watched every day, wondering at times if knowing that family and friends are watching your every move might not take a little away from the freedom of wandering through such a wilderness on your own. But I was quite gratified and not a little flattered when I got back to England and heard from so many people that they had enjoyed following the journey.

superb spot, soft and grassy, right next to a little babbling brook and kitted out with bear lockers to put away your food and, oddly, anything scented.

I had made it up there exactly on schedule although I had needed to put in a pretty relentless seven days to get there on time for my camping permit and, since there was only me and a man and his young son at the site, I wondered why the Saguaro National Park insists on making it quite so complicated for people to camp there. Perhaps the answer lies in America's great anomaly – that in the Land of the Free, when it comes to the nation's public bodies, there are such a bewildering multitude of rules and regulations that life is often far from free for its citizens.

Day 8, Grass Shack Camp to The Lakes, 20 miles

This was a day of real highs and lows, in more ways than one. Refreshed by Pop C's supper and a pleasantly quiet and, I am pleased to report, bear-free night, I made great progress up towards the top of the Rincons, 3200ft above Grass Shack Camp. The morning was delightfully cool and as the pinon pines and oaks gave way to ponderosa pines and Douglas firs on the higher slopes, the air became heavy with the invigorating scent of the forest. The views back to the south were spectacular and as 3000ft climbs go, that was one of the easiest I can remember.

By midday I was over the ridge and ready to tackle the near 5,000ft descent on the north side of the Rincons. The trail immediately became almost impossible to follow – much of the narrow track was covered in snow and there were shrubs and fire damaged trees lying across it everywhere. I decided to follow it very, very carefully knowing that if I lost my way for a moment, there would be no chance of finding the trail again. But lose it is exactly what I did. Just after passing the deeply disappointing Italian Spring, a small green, muddy hole in the ground, the path seemed to disappear totally into a deep thicket.

For more than an hour I cast round in ever increasing circles, bush-whacking up and down the steep and snowy slope. Finally I made the reluctant decision, remembering the harsh lesson learned from my disastrous episode in the Superstitions, that if I tried to find my own way down such a long and steep mountainside, I could get myself into a lot of trouble. Reluctantly I concluded that the only thing to do was to climb back up to the ridge, retrace my steps back down the south side of the Rincons and walk round the mountain range. It would probably lose me a couple of days but I honestly could not see any other option.

Then, miraculously, just as I returned for the umpteenth time to the place where I had lost the trail, there it was, clear as you like, heading down the east side of the ridge. With huge relief I resumed my tortuous descent, the snow and fire damage quickly disappeared and, I have to say, it really was a very nice and quite wide path. How I had failed to spot it earlier perplexes me to this day.

As I reached the dry grasslands at the base of the Rincons, a stiff wind blew up and I spent a long time moving on through the rocky hills looking for a flat, sheltered and stone free campsite. It was nearly dark by the time I threw down my pack and pitched camp in a sandy wash, right across the Arizona Trail. Still, I was a great deal closer to the base of the next day's target, Mt Lemmon, and I had high hopes of a late lunch at the pleasantly named ski resort of Summerhaven. Altogether I had climbed 4,000ft and descended 6,000ft that day and with my bushwhacking episode, possible a good bit more.

Day 9, The Lakes to below Summerhaven, 22 miles

I had set myself a very tough challenge in trying to get up to Summerhaven by mid afternoon so I made my earliest start so far, breaking camp as soon as the sun came up. The great bulk of Mt Lemmon and the Santa Catalinas loomed ever closer but first there was an unexpected 1000ft climb over a hill so small it was apparently hardly worth showing on my map.

63

The climb began in earnest several miles beyond and more than 1000ft lower. There is nothing more irritating than making a big descent when you can see a very eye catching climb just ahead of you, but when the climb up Mt Lemmon's west side really kicked off it was unremittingly steep, rocky and tortuous, ascending more than 4,000ft in less than 10 miles. The views back to the Rincons and nearby Tucson were magnificent and this was by a distance the most spectacular mountain I had yet seen with huge rock columns bursting out of the earth all around. One day I will go back there and climb it with a little less haste and enjoy it more.

Just past midday the weather began to change alarmingly as clouds gathered high above Mount Lemmon. The wind had picked up quite sharply and as I climbed higher and higher it became distinctly chilly. Seemingly from nowhere appeared the ski resort of Summerhaven, the place where people from Phoenix and, more especially, Tucson like to go in summer to cool off. It is one of three ski resorts in Arizona, which perhaps says a great deal for America's unquenchable spirit of optimism.

Not many years ago a huge fire ripped through the entire community leaving behind nothing but burnt out Alpine chalets and huge charred pine trunks. The latter are still in place but the former are being rebuilt with the enthusiasm of Ireland in its Celtic Tiger years. It gave the entire place the appearance less of a resort than of a giant building site and the chill wind and grey sky did little to cheer things up.

But joyously I had made it in time to catch Cookies, which serves biscuits the size of dinner plates and home made pizzas. I ordered the smallest cookie on offer to save for a treat later and a 7" pizza. The owner, who had already established my hungry hiker credentials, looked disappointed as he confirmed "Just the seven inch?", perhaps wanting to add "not the 12 inch, the 15 inch or one the size of a Mexican's hat?" I almost gave in from shame.

When the pizza arrived I was glad I had stuck to my guns. As well as being seven inches wide it was about seven inches deep, loaded with all the vegetables my diet had been sorely lacking since

Rebuilding Summerhaven

Patagonia and quite delicious. The chalet was filling up with racing cyclists from a training camp in Tucson. First up the mountain was a girl no more than five foot tall but with hugely powerful legs of almost the same circumference. The rest rolled in well behind, ashen and sweating profusely from the 5,000ft straight up climb. I envied them their bikes but not the chilly and steep descent down the mountain. Cycling friends will confirm that I am the world's most pathetic descender, usually arriving at the bottom of a mountain with smoke billowing from my brake blocks just as my companions are half way through lunch.

I finished my pizza and three cups of tea and waddled off reluctantly down the road, very full and happy. But by now it was becoming seriously gloomy outside, bitterly cold and extremely windy. Bits of stray rubbish were blowing wildly around Summerhaven. I headed for the Oracle Ridge which pretty much does what it says on the tin, leading steeply down to the town of Oracle 17 miles away.

Half a mile along and I knew that attempting the Oracle Ridge that afternoon was going to be a very bad idea indeed. The wind was absolutely howling across the spine of the mountain and dark clouds were swirling all around. With sharp drops on both sides and 50 mph gusts buffeting me from side to side any further progress would have been exceptionally foolish. I headed back up to the top of the trail to have a rethink. With a storm coming down fast, I needed to get as far down the mountain as possible before nightfall.

My good old paper map showed what appeared to be a forest road heading down towards Oracle and I sought it out immediately. The good news was that I had found a splendid track; wide, firm and contouring gently down through the forest. The bad news was a sign at the top announcing Oracle 29, twelve miles further than the ridgeline, but I decided that the extra miles would be a small price to pay for not killing myself in an untidy fall off the mountain or getting caught in a storm at the top of Mount Lemmon. I barely hesitated a moment before heading off smartly down the mountain towards "Oracle 29".

Storm coming down on Mount Lemmon

Day 10, Slopes of Mount Lemmon to Oracle, 26 miles

I camped a few miles down the track after searching well into the dusk to find somewhere reasonably sheltered from the strong wind. I clearly failed in the latter aim when my tent comprehensively came down around my ears at midnight. I got up and moved it round so that the back of the tent pointed into the wind and that seemed to work to some extent but it was an exceptionally wild and windy night and in the small hours snow and little pellets of ice fell for about ten minutes. My decision to get off the ridgeline was looking better and better.

Oracle beckoned and I set off very early again. The track was a great piece of road building but frustrating to walk, its end-less switchbacks turning 12 miles as the crow flies into a slightly monotonous 29. Further down I passed a dude ranch where wealthy weekenders could come and play at being cowboys for a couple of days and a little beyond, Peppersauce Camp, a sizeable campground with absolutely nobody in it apart from the camp supervisor washing pans outside a rather dismal looking mobilehome.

I asked him how far it was to Oracle and he replied bizarrely, "Ten miles, 45 minutes". "Which is it?" I asked. "Both", he replied. I pointed out that I would need a vehicle to get there in 45 minutes but he said he had a friend who could do it on foot in 45 minutes. I gave up – either he was as mad as a box of frogs or Mo Farah was his best mate. I thanked him for a fill up of water and carried on my way.

Ten miles and three hours later I made it to Oracle, or at least a part of Oracle. Clearly land was not at a premium around those parts and over the next few hours I would clock up many more miles trekking between the little towns's amazingly spread out facilities. First of all I looked in at the eerily deserted Oracle Chalet Village which was clearly open for business but unattended. I headed back up the road to eat a burger, collect my post box and check e-mails at the library. There were absolutely no e-mails in my in-box, nor would there be until nearly a month later due to yet another glitch in my personal e-mail address. I was well and truly out of touch.

I picked up some shopping at the Oracle Market, which was not really a market at all but a rather modest little supermarket, and trudged back up the road to the Oracle Chalet Village, which still showed no signs of life. I settled down with a book in the late afternoon sun, reasoning that someone would surely turn up eventually. Not much later Marnie, the owner showed up and gave me a very decent room at a ridiculously cheap price.

Marnie could not have been more accommodating – no, not in that way, you dirty-minded fools! She loved having thru-hikers stay at her motel but said that quite a number arrived at Oracle in poor shape and gave up. She kept a box of all sorts of odds and ends left behind by Arizona Trail hikers from which I helped myself to a big bag of trail mix and some shampoo and a comb to try and restore order to my unkempt locks. All that and a comfortable room for the night and the use of a washing machine for just $30.

Spruced up after seven straight days out on the trail and with clean clothes as well, I treated myself to a substantial dinner at a little Mexican restaurant half a mile up the road. The meal cost me just $7.49 plus the cost of a large bottle of beer from the petrol station opposite and it was absolutely delicious. When I left at 7.30 I was the last one there by nearly half an hour and I couldn't help noticing how Americans like to eat out with no ceremony whatsoever, throwing food down their necks in double quick time, usually without anything to drink besides water, pay their bill whilst they are still eating and leave as soon as the last forkful has been shoved in. Mind you, perhaps at $7.49 for a veritable feast you don't need to treat eating out as a special occasion.

EDWARD ABBEY

Months before my trip I had hoped to visit the house of the legendary author and environmental activist who is usually said to have died at his home in Oracle in 1989. But just before going out to Arizona I read James Cahalan's worthy and thorough, if somewhat ponderous biography of Abbey and it is clear that he never in fact lived at Oracle and certainly did not die there. In reality Edward Abbey's only connection with the town seems to be that when he became successful and famous he kept a post box there and even advertised its address on dust jackets to throw people off track from his real address west of Tucson. In that way he could only be found by people he wanted to be found by.

I can thoroughly recommend reading some Edward Abbey. He is an exceptional writer. It is not all good, nor will you agree with everything he says. I sometimes wonder if even he agreed with everything he said. Some of what he wrote was probably just written to get a reaction and make his readers think a little but you will constantly come across passages of utter brilliance. His autobiographical "Desert Solitaire" is a good place to start or his famous novel "The Monkey Wrench Gang", one of modern American literature's most famous books never to be filmed. Hollywood probably just could not get its head around a story which set environmental terrorists at its heart. One of its central characters, George Hayduke, now has a long distance hiking trail named after him which winds through most of southern Utah's most remote wilderness for some 750 miles.

Chapter 7

PRICKS IN MY BUM

ORACLE TO SUPERIOR, 88 MILES

"The world is full of cactus, but we don't have to sit on it"
Will Foley

Day 11, Oracle to Antelope Peak, 19 miles

If I had been nervous about crossing the Rincons and Mount Lemmon, the next fifty miles due north across the flat, open Sonoran Desert as far as the Gila River had given me sleepless nights since I first heard about the drought conditions around Phoenix. However many times I looked at the trail notes, there appeared to be vast tracts of land on my route for the next three days without any water sources at all.

So after a slightly disappointing breakfast of coffee and a cheese and cherry Danish pastry (yes, that was cheese and cherry) gleaned from the best that the Oracle Market had to offer, I set off with my pack laden with as much water as I could carry. I also made what would prove to be the first of three self inflicted mistakes that day by adding a 4 pint container of milk to my load.

Why, you may ask, was I carrying half a gallon of milk, which wouldn't keep more than half a day in the desert heat? Well, mostly because I needed an extra drinks container for this dry section and also because it would give me something better to drink that morning other than plain old water. I didn't much fancy the supermarket's other alternative, half a gallon of the sugary concoctions that

70

▲ *Legs among the lupins*

▼ *Disappearing trail in Sonoran Desert flowers*

passed for fruit juices.

I will spare you the details, which might be more information than you need. Suffice it to say that I spent a good part of the day trotting off the trail to satisfy the demands of an over-active digestive system. Remembering that the same thing had happened to me after leaving Patagonia, also with four pints of milk hanging from my pack, it was becoming clear that I must have some kind of lactose intolerance. Since this unexpected discovery I haven't given up milk in the ten or so cups of tea that help me get through the day but I no longer skull the white stuff by the mug full.

The Sonoran desert was unexpectedly verdant and quite beautiful. The snows of a fortnight before had left the arid landscape with a lush green carpet and an ample profusion of little flowers, mostly yellow. Try as I might I could not identify them from the six or so pages of similar looking yellow wildflowers in the Audubon Guide so I can't tell you what they were called but the overall effect was very lovely and most surprising.

Lovely that is if you were not trying to find the Arizona Trail through the middle of it all. The new growth made the trail, which in any case was little more than a scratch in the sand, well-nigh impossible to see and I constantly lost it, although the surrounding desert was so flat and easy to cross that it did not matter much.

ROUTE FINDING

With a few notable exceptions route finding was mostly not too difficult, although throughout the journey I constantly lost the Arizona Trail, seldom for too long though. Maybe I was used to British paths, which are generally quite easy to follow, but in the hard, rocky terrain of Arizona, the trail was often little more than a slightly different arrangement of stones. Sometimes little stone cairns had been made and I could navigate from one to the next, but they were often quite tricky to spot and occasionally the next cairn would be hidden behind a bush, which was far

---

from helpful.

I carried maps of the trail beautifully printed for me on water-proof paper by a friend in Norfolk but at half an inch to the mile, they left something to be desired compared to the wonderfully intricate detail of British Ordnance Survey maps. In addition I had the Arizona Trail Association's trail notes which gave all sorts of information, including water sources and altitudes, which I could tie in with my Timex WS4 altimeter watch. The watch was a little complicated but extremely useful and also featured a compass and temperature gauge, although the altitude did need resetting rather more often than I might have hoped. I didn't carry a GPS, partly because I am completely hopeless with gadgets but mostly because I prefer the greater scope of a map. If I can get away doing things the old school way, then I always will.

Generally, although the actual trail was often extraordinarily difficult to see, getting to my next destination never was. Being able to see the next sky island meant that I could always make that a target and if all else failed, I just had to keep heading north. If the sun was shining and I couldn't see my shadow on the ground in front, then I wasn't heading north.

My second piece of foolishness came around midday when I decided to get out my camcorder and do some self filming amongst the desert flowers. I picked a spot particularly verdant with blooms, carefully set up the camcorder on my Gorilla Pod, aimed it at an especially picturesque cholla cactus and sat down on the desert floor. Now the one thing you need to know about the cholla cactus, and which I had momentarily forgotten, is that they constantly shed their spines in little clumps about the size of a golf ball.

Needless to say, on a list of *Things Not to Do in the Desert*, sitting down under a cholla cactus comes pretty near the top. I shot up about three feet in the air and jumped around a great deal fouling the clean desert air with some choice Anglo Saxon. Not surprisingly, filming was abandoned in favour of a not wholly successful fifteen minutes spent extracting cactus spines from my shorts and my nether regions.

Perhaps because of this episode and the other bottom trouble I was suffering from, my concentration wavered and I soon lost the trail completely and wandered off into a vast area of thick cacti of all varieties; yucca, prickly pear, saguaro and my old friend the cholla, in several different guises. They were so dense that there was absolutely no way of avoiding getting scratched all over my bare legs and arms. Worse still, my pack and my fleece, which was hanging loose off my pack, picked up dozens of tiny barbed spines which I was still picking out days later. Every time I put my fleece on until I next washed it in Superior I managed to transfer more little spines into the skin of my back and shoulders.

Then suddenly and miraculously, after a couple of miles of painful bushwhacking, I emerged from the cactus forest exactly where I wanted to be. Not long after, I found my first water of the day in a murky looking cattle tank and made camp in a lovely, sheltered wash just before Antelope Peak, a bare volcanic looking hill that resembled some that I have climbed or cycled up in Lanzarote. I settled down gratefully for a good night's sleep, hopeful that if mishaps came in threes, I might be safe for a while.

Day 12, Antelope Peak to The Big Hill, 25 miles

After a superb night's sleep I found myself making something of an unplanned early getaway. At seven o'clock a pick-up truck came by on a track a couple of hundred yards away, the first sign of human life I had seen anywhere in the Sonoran Desert. I was a little concerned that I might have camped on private land. I was probably half a mile or so from the Arizona Trail and all around the area were signs of ranch activity, cattle tanks, fences and stockades and, yes, the occasional cow.

The pick-up stopped, backed up a bit then waited a few minutes and

74

drove away only to return a few minutes later and wait nearby again. The occupants may just have been having their breakfast but I did not much want a lively discussion along the lines of "What the hell are you doing on my land?" with an angry and most likely armed rancher, so I packed up with more than my usual speed and cleared off without any breakfast.

I made some good miles across mostly flat terrain. The trail was excellent all day and better still, I managed not to lose it once. Water was a huge worry though as it was around 30 miles from my overnight camp to the next place where I could be sure of finding water. There was a chance of finding a public water cache at the Freeman Road Trailhead but it was marked on the trail maps as W0, meaning "Water not reliable". If there wasn't any there, I would have to divert to one of the old mining towns 10 miles to the east. But sure enough, at the Freeman Road Trailhead was a neat little wooden cabinet filled with plastic water containers helpfully left there for hikers. A real life saver.

The only cloud on the horizon was a problem that would haunt me for the next week and threatened to completely derail the walk. My feet had settled down well after the problems of the first week. The blisters had all healed and no further difficulties had cropped up. Perhaps my feet just needed some time to get used to the punishment or maybe they appreciated the Vaseline that I would carefully rub on them before putting my socks on in the morning and again in the evening before changing into my thick, thermal camp socks.

But after just 250 miles I noticed that the soles of my boots were already going through alarmingly fast; the fantastically comfortable Hoka One One hiking boots from France that I had expected to last until Flagstaff, where I knew I could replace them, or at worst Pine where I might possibly find another pair. I couldn't blame the boots, which were lightweight, lavishly cushioned and as comfortable as you could wish for. They just were not designed for the brutally hard and sharp rock that I had been walking over thus far.

I now had to make a big decision. When I reached the Gila River the following morning, should I go up the main road to Superior and

▲ *Dead Saguaro Cactus*

▼ *Camping across the trail*

replace them with whatever I could find there? If there wasn't anything there I would have to make my way to Phoenix and get something decent. Or should I take a chance on them holding together whilst I continued west along the Gila River then through the White Canyon Wilderness to arrive in Superior by the proper route. I mulled over the problem that evening and decided to let valour be the better part of discretion and plough on along the Arizona Trail to Superior with my rapidly disintegrating boots.

Day 13, The Big Hill to Walnut Canyon, 22 miles

I woke up that morning from a deep sleep. I had been dreaming that I wanted to enter a race but didn't have any running shoes. I went into a tiny village shop to try and buy some and the assistant said that he thought he had one pair left. He disappeared into the back of the shop only to return with a pair of wooden clogs. Footwear would be constantly in my thoughts for the whole of the next week.

I was hoping to press on and make Superior by the next evening and planned to stay there for two nights. The effort of doing twenty miles or more every day was starting to take its toll and two nights off the trail might help to put some fuel back in the tank. Also, if Superior proved to be boot free, I would need most of the day to get into Phoenix and back. I needed to squeeze about 45 miles out of the next two days but the morning's walking along the western edge of the low Tortilla Mountains proved to be hillier than expected and I also lost the trail for a while and had to backtrack for nearly a mile.

All the while the views ahead were spectacular as the flat Sonoran Desert gave way to the White Canyon Wilderness ahead and the massive bulk of the Superstition Mountains beyond. To the North West I could see clearly the ugly blue green scar of the huge open cast copper mine near Ray. It was quite a sight but a disturbing contrast to the pristine wilderness I was walking through. Copper mining had been going on in the area since 1947 and it was just about the only reason for the existence of several small towns along the San Pedro River. With world copper prices currently at a high,

77

the giant ASARCO mine is having something of a revival.

At noon I reached the small town of Kelvin at the point where the trail meets the Gila River. A quick inspection revealed that there was absolutely nothing in Kelvin that was of interest to a tired and hungry hiker – no shop or gas station, nothing apart from the river, a nice looking bridge, a couple of hundred houses and a trailer park. I badly needed water and although there was clearly plenty of it in the river, the trail notes warned that it might be contaminated - in fact ASARCO had been prosecuted in 1997 for dumping arsenic, lead and copper into the river, none of which I particularly wanted in my water bottles.

Instead hikers were supposed to use a faucet (tap) at the maintenance depot just across the river but that was closed and my feeble attempts to climb over the fence came to nothing. I trudged on to a dreadful looking trailer park half a mile up the road where there was no sign of life apart from a few unpleasant looking dogs thankfully tied up with stout chains. I knocked on the door of a respectable clapboard house nearby but there was no reply so I nosed round the back looking for a tap I could use. An old lady with a kindly face appeared at the back door of the house and said I could use a faucet at the side of the house.

I realised that she had been the first person I had spoken to for over two days and wondered if she had people to talk to herself. I hoped that she had someone looking out for her – an isolated community in America is not the place to be if you do not have a car.

The brand new Arizona Trail along the Gila River was superb, though for a river route it was far from flat. Over and over again it wound in and out of the small canyons which cut into the hills to the north of the brown, slow flowing river affording wonderful views of the Sonoran Desert to the south and the jagged peaks of the White Canyon Wilderness to the north.

I ran into a young couple from Phoenix who were hiking the Arizona Trail in bite sized sections. I hadn't seen anyone on foot on the trail since my encounter with Pop C nearly a week before. We

Mining railway bridge over the Gila River

all sat down and chatted about trail matters, enjoying an unscheduled rest and some time out of the hot sun. They were very encouraging about the water situation just along the trail, less so about the amount of snow that had fallen beyond Pine. All being well I should reach there in less than ten days.

TOMATO OR TOMAYTO ?

My encounter with the old lady and her faucet at Kelvin made me realise that a visit to America involves getting used to a whole new set of words. If you don't use the American word, people will look blankly at you as if you had just broken out into Swedish. There is absolutely no point in using familiar English words like petrol, pavement, lift, bonnet or boot. Instead you must learn to use gas, sidewalk, elevator, hood and trunk.

And so it is with walking terms. Americans don't walk, they hike and if they are doing the whole thing, it is called a thru-hike. Now to me hiking always brings to mind something that Enid Blyton's Famous Five might have done, probably in corduroy shorts and Aertex shirts and carrying a canvas knapsack filled with "lashings of ginger beer". Most British walkers call themselves just that - walkers.

In Britain we walk on a path, perhaps a track if it is a bit wider but Americans hike on a trail. Our paths often pass through valleys but in the States, particularly in the south west, a valley is always called a canyon, whether it is grand or not. A dried up stream bed is a wash and if I wanted to fill my water bottles I would need to ask for a faucet instead of a tap.

I learned pretty quickly but, dear reader, you will have to forgive me if I slip seamlessly and pointlessly between American and English. Oh, and if you ever want to cadge a cigarette from an American, just don't ask him if you can bum a fag.

Day 14, Walnut Canyon to Superior, 25 miles

After a pleasant night spent close to the Gila River at my lowest campsite of the entire journey, a mere 1700ft, I pushed on hard to reach Superior by late afternoon for my planned two nights of recuperation and boot shopping. I would need to put in a good day's walking. Superior was 25 miles away.

Three miles along the river, the trail abruptly turned north to head up into the White Canyon Wilderness on a brand new section of trail. For the next nine miles I enjoyed the best scenery I had seen so far on a new section of trail that often just seemed to be carved straight out of the side of the mountains. Everywhere were the sharp canyons, mesa and buttes of the White Canyon, all in fantastic shades of red, yellow and green. There were wild flowers everywhere after the recent snows. The only thing missing to complete the picture were the famous bighorn sheep which were reputed to inhabit the area.

Saguaros in the White Canyon Wilderness

Although the trail only climbed up to 3800ft, it often felt much higher. It was the sort of trail that was really quite safe but you needed to pay attention at all times; one small stumble might send you slithering down a 1 in 2 slope covered in sharp rocks and prickly bushes, hoping that your fall might be arrested by a small tree. Not a great prospect and one that I took great pains to avoid. Surprisingly for a trail that was only an hour or so from Phoenix and was unbelievably stunning I saw no other hikers at all and just one mountain biker going at a tremendous rate.

I made it into Superior around four o'clock, booked in at the Copper Mountain Motel for two nights and wandered out into the town for a quick look at just what Superior might have to offer both in terms of resupply and boot replacement. A couple of miles later and it was quite clear that, interesting though the old town might be, it did not sell any kind of footwear whatsoever, let alone a useable pair of hiking boots. Furthermore, if I wanted to get into Phoenix to buy some, there was no bus or taxi service to take me there and to further fill my cup of happiness to overflowing, there appeared not to be a computer I could use in town. The day being Saturday, the library would be closed until Monday.

Troy, the manager of the Copper Mountain Motel, came over all jobsworth when I asked him if I might be able to send a quick e-mail or two from the motel's computer, telling me that under no circumstances whatsoever would the owners allow that. Thankfully the next morning he relented and I was able to send off a couple of quick messages.

But that evening I felt a bit stuck all round and wondered if I might have to push on with my disintegrating footwear all the way to Pine, 150 miles away across three huge mountain ranges; the Superstitions, the Four Peaks Wilderness and the Mazatzals. Looking at my boots, I think I might have been barefoot by the time I got there.

I cheered myself up greatly by laundering my clothes, taking a much needed shower and enjoying a Mexican meal every bit the equal of the $7.49 feast I had gorged myself on in Oracle and, despite the addition of a couple of refreshing bottles of beer, not much more expensive. Bright lights, terrible décor and the peculiar Formica topped tables that are such an odd feature of eateries in a country that has so many forests, yet the place was heaving, mostly with women and families. Small town good cheer abounded with waitresses and customers alike having one big party. But it was not my party so I headed back up the road to the Copper Mountain Motel and just past nine o'clock settled down for some much needed rest in a comfortable bed. I would take another look at my boot shopping options in the morning.

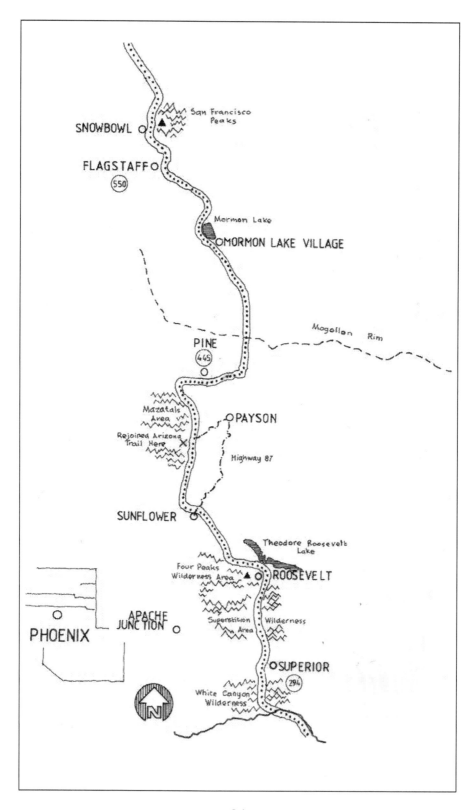

San Francisco Peaks

SNOWBOWL

FLAGSTAFF
550

Mormon Lake

MORMON LAKE VILLAGE

Mogollon Rim

PINE
445

Mazatals Area

PAYSON

Rejoined Arizona Trail Here

Highway 87

SUNFLOWER

Theodore Roosevelt Lake

Four Peaks Wilderness Area

ROOSEVELT

Superstition Area

Wilderness

APACHE JUNCTION

PHOENIX

SUPERIOR
294

White Canyon Wilderness

N

Chapter 8

TESTED TO THE LIMIT

SUPERIOR TO PINE, 140 MILES

*"There is a phenomenon called Trail Magic, known and spoken of
with reverence by everyone who hikes the trail, which holds that
often when things look darkest, some little piece of serendipity
comes along to put you back on a heavenly plane"*
Bill Bryson, A Walk in the Woods

Day 15, Superior to Whitford Canyon, 6 miles

I had an appalling night's sleep at the Copper Mountain Motel.
Whoever was in the next door room had the television on all through
the night at top volume. The television was tuned into a station
playing old movies and Bette Davis, Humphrey Bogart and Ingrid
Bergman amongst many others were coming through the wall loud
and clear until I finally gave up on any idea of a proper sleep and got
up around 5 o'clock to clean and sort through my kit.

Several times I thought about knocking on the door and letting the
occupants know the error of their ways but I reckoned I didn't want
to risk being the headline in Monday's Arizona Star, "Lone Brit
Hiker Killed in Motel Shooting" and so suffered in silence.

Later that morning through gritted teeth I had a very pleasant chat
with a single man who emerged from the next door room around
11 o'clock and told me that he had arrived at the motel last night so
tired that he had slept right round the clock. He had obviously fallen

asleep with the television on, a fact that seemed to have passed him by. Well good for you, I thought, and in true British fashion said absolutely nothing about my disturbed night.

At 7.30 I wandered off into the old (circa 1900) bit of Superior in search of some early breakfast. The housing and shops of the old town had a somewhat forlorn air about them and you could see why the very real decrepitude of Superior's downtown area had been so much in demand by film directors for years. *How the West Was Won* was shot there and in reviewing Oliver Stone's *U-Turn*, one movie critic described Superior as looking like "one of those backwater hells where everyone is malevolent, over-sexed, narrow-eyed and hateful".

As I enjoyed an excellent breakfast served by a pretty waitress who was neither malevolent, hateful nor narrow–eyed and also, sadly, not over-sexed, I thought that the movie critic's comments were a little unfair. There was much to commend about the spirit and friendliness of Superior and I would have loved to have been there the following week when the annual Apache Leap Mining Festival was due to be held. The town had gone through more boom and busts than the British economy. First springing up around a somewhat fickle silver mine, things really took off when silver dried up at the nearby town of Pinal and copper was discovered at Superior. The good folk of Pinal simply upped sticks and moved up the road, possibly bringing much of their town with them.

Now Superior may be about to enjoy a new boom. More copper has been discovered, enough apparently to supply 25% of America's copper needs and a copper mining company has opened a swanky new office in one of the old shops. But you can bet your life that the new breed of miner won't be interested in refurbishing the lovely old clapboard houses that were for sale everywhere. They will probably build a new enclave on the edge of town and a Walmart will appear in no time at all, further adding to the decline of the old town.

Another fractured night's sleep at the Copper Mountain was a risk I wasn't prepared to take and over breakfast I made a plan to head towards Phoenix, buy some new boots and get back out on the trail that afternoon. I packed up my gear and checked out of the Motel, finding Troy in a much better humour – not only did he allow me to use the Motel's computer but he also let me off paying for the second night.

Midday saw me hanging around outside a restroom area on the edge of town trying to cadge a ride from the few motorists who happened to be both desperate for a pee and heading Phoenix way. I rather think that my by now long and wild hair and straggly beard might have put most people off, that and the fact that I was accosting unwary drivers as they emerged from the restrooms. At any rate I was still there two hours later and about to give up and have a rethink when Jim and Mary, two snowbirds from North Dakota, decided to take pity on the scruffy Englishman. They were heading down towards Tucson for the afternoon but decided to change their plans and go there some other time just so that they could drop me off at Walmart in Apache Junction.

Thundering up Highway 60 to be deposited back in Apache Junction felt very strange indeed. After more than two largely solitary weeks I was back amongst big crowds of people. Not only that but I was only a mile or so away from the place where not long ago I had been enjoying a family holiday of loafing by the pool, playing golf and tucking into big barbecues.

End of the road for my Hoka One Ones

A big Walmart makes the average British supermarket look like a small corner shop. You can buy everything there from around 200 different types of breakfast cereal to enough weaponry to start a civil war in a small West African republic. What they did not have though was a good selection of trail boots. The choice was pretty much take it or leave it. So I took it, a pair of optimistically named Ozark Trail Boots, circa 1980 spec, heavy as hell and with little or no cushioning in the tread. But they looked sound enough and I thought, "What the heck, at $20 and if they get me to Flagstaff, I'll be happy."

Outside I called a taxi with the aid of a couple of amazingly helpful Walmart staff, one of whom not only found the number of a taxi firm for me but lent me his phone to call them. Whilst I waited, I sat on the pavement and put my new boots on, stuffing the box and my battered Hoka One Ones into a bin.

Nearby I caught site of a couple of mothers and their young daughters examining with amazement and not a little trepidation the odd sight of a wild haired man throwing his boots in a bin. They were running one of the popular Girl Guide Cookie stalls that you see all over retail America at weekends. I felt obliged to go over and explain myself and also to add a packet of $4 mint chocolate cookies to my already bulging pack.

Soon Kyle from the Green Cab Company was there to whisk me back to Superior. Like so many, Kyle had moved to Arizona from another state but I got the feeling that things had not gone that well for him which was why he was now driving a cab. He cautioned me against going up into the Superstitions suggesting that it was "full of rattlesnakes, scorpions and wackos with guns".

Late on a very hot afternoon indeed, and the forecast for the next couple of days was in the high 80s, I got back on the trail at the Picketpost Trailhead, putting in another six miles across some fairly flat terrain before making a lovely camp underneath the Superstition Wilderness, my target for the next day.

TRAILHEADS

All along the trail I would go through or close to trailheads, often with splendidly exotic names like Picketpost, American Flag or Lone Pine Saddle. Naively I somehow always expected to find something interesting at them, perhaps a kiosk selling food or even a washroom with running water but I was always disappointed.

They were just places near roads for people to leave their vehicles so that they could head off into the wilderness on foot, or by bike, horse or even quad bike. Apart from a couple of times when I saw day hikers getting back into their vehicles, I never once found anything more interesting at a trailhead than a board displaying a map of the Arizona Trail.

Day 16, Whitford Canyon to Reavis Saddle, 18 miles

After my adventure in the Superstitions three weeks before, I needed to up my game a bit for my next visit to the mountains, but for a range in which the highest summits only reach 6,000ft, they were to prove exceptionally difficult to cross. Although not particularly high, they are steep and sharp and riddled with a complex web of canyons, peaks and ridges. One look at a map of the mountains reveals tightly packed contour lines and few trees, a harsh and unforgiving place to walk through.

Although it is now a fabulous, isolated wilderness the Superstition Mountains probably have more legends attached to them than almost anywhere in America. In fact Superstition myths have spawned a whole industry and in one tourist centre just outside Apache Junction I counted no fewer than 25 books on the history and legends of the mountains.

What is alleged to have happened, and alleged is perhaps the most important word in the story, gave rise to the legend of The Lost Dutchman Gold Mine. It all started when a prospector called Jacob Waltz, who probably wasn't Dutch at all but German, was rumoured to have found an old Spanish gold mine in the Superstitions. Thereafter he was reputed to have made numerous trips into the mountains, each time returning with bags of gold. But he would never tell anyone where the gold came from and seems to have shot several people who tried to follow him. After Waltz's death in 1891 there was much local speculation about the legendary lost gold mine, especially after the splendidly named journalist Pierpont Constable Bicknell got hold of the story and claimed that Waltz had left behind a map of the mine's location and furthermore that gold had been found under his bed when he died.

But the whole thing had been largely consigned to history until the 1930s when an elderly treasure hunter from Washington D.C. called Dr Adolph Ruth turned up at Apache Junction claiming to have a map of the mine. He ventured into the Superstitions and was never seen alive again, though his skull was found months later with a bullet wound in it. Since then the interest has never died down and to this day people go up into the mountains in search of the Lost Dutchman Gold Mine, convinced that it is still there. There are whole websites devoted to the mystery, tee-shirts, books, treasure maps, even a Lost Dutchman Marathon each year at Apache Junction.

But I was climbing up into the Superstitions not to seek my fortune but just to get to the other side without a major mishap. The 3,000ft climb felt tough, even though I spent much of it on a wide, easy to follow track – so wide in fact that late in the morning I found myself sharing it with what appeared to be a quad bike safari, ten of the noisy things shattering the peace of the foothills. Disappointingly for a climb that was not especially steep, I was making hard work of it and I began to worry that with much bigger and steeper challenges ahead, particularly in the Four Peaks Wilderness and the Mazatzals, my body might be running out of steam. Perhaps the extra night in Superior would have been a good idea after all. The consolation lay in the wonderful views of the Superstitions ahead and looking back I could clearly see Mount Lemmon, which I had crossed six days before.

The night in Superior had also made me realise that I was losing weight at a prodigious rate. In my motel room I caught sight of myself in a mirror and had to do a bit of a double take. Ribs that I had not seen for twenty years were showing through and my hip bones were sticking out too. Later I would find that I had lost an alarming 21lbs in just three weeks. Really it was not particularly surprising if I thought about my diet. Whilst I was burning at least 4000 calories each day through ten hours of hard walking, the meagre provisions I could carry between resupply towns meant that I was taking on board less than 1500. Clearly that was not nearly enough to sustain the effort but with up to seven days' food to be carried on my back, I could not see how I could bring any more away from the towns. Still, I resolved to do better with my diet wherever possible.

Soon I crested a ridge, left the noisy quad bikes behind and reached the official start of the Superstition Wilderness at the Rogers Trough Trailhead. I had not seen another hiker since meeting the couple by the Gila River two days earlier and now suddenly there were twenty, a party of day hikers from Phoenix who had just walked a few rocky miles along the trail to see some 600 year old cave dwellings. They kindly offered me some much needed water and a Power Bar, both of which I gratefully accepted. Also at the trailhead was a man with a large RV and speaker system to match from which could be heard a radio station dedicated to rock music, played at an attention grabbing volume. Quite how he had managed to get such a large vehicle up the track to the trailhead was something of a mystery.

Beyond Rogers Trough the trail deteriorated alarmingly and soon became rocky, narrow and overgrown with profuse, hard-stemmed shrubs which grew in on either side. I ran into a party of students, members of the Southwestern Volunteer Corps who were working hard on fixing the path, and boy, did it need fixing.

That night was my warmest yet, for which I was extremely grateful. I was somewhat less grateful for the strengthening wind turning round through 180 degrees in the middle of the night. I couldn't be bothered to repitch my tent and so just took it down and slept on top of it. After that night I found that I rather preferred to sleep in the open and only put my tent up a couple of times on the rest of the journey, preferring to just use it as a groundsheet and sleep out in the open enjoying the clear night sky.

Day 17, Reavis Saddle to Cottonwood Camp, 20 miles

This was Reavis Country – I was on the Reavis Ranch Trail and a glance at the map revealed a Reavis Canyon, Ranch, Saddle, Spring, Gap, Valley, Creek and on the eastern boundary of the Superstition Wilderness, a Reavis Mountain School. They were all named after one Elishah M Reavis. In the late 19th century at a time when practically no one thought it worth going up into the Superstitions aside from a few optimistic prospectors, he decided to settle there and, somewhat improbably, grow fruit and vegetables which he shipped out to markets in the mining towns springing up on the flatter lands below. A famous photograph of the man who lived something of a hermit-like existence so high up in the hills shows a wild looking, dark-faced man with just about the longest, most tangled beard you will ever see. If you don't believe me, Google him.

Not for first time I broke camp without any breakfast. The mornings were mostly so cold that with frozen fingers I often struggled just to pack up my kit and bothering to wait for freezing water to boil seemed like too much trouble altogether. As the journey progressed and I became less and less enamoured with the freezing cold mornings, I got into the habit of doing a few miles to get warm before making some porridge and coffee. My plan was to stop a few miles along the trail and brew up at the site of the old Reavis Ranch.

It was a fascinating spot, right in the middle of just about the only flat valley in the mountains and with a pleasant stream running through it. Green, lush and verdant with plenty of grass and healthy looking trees, you could see why Elishah Reavis had chosen the location. The remains of what must once have been quite a large house were clearly visible with the majority of a substantial tiled floor still in place. Nearby I found the axle of a sizeable piece of machinery made by a Connecticut manufacturer.

Early morning brew-up at Reavis Ranch

How anyone could have got a heavy thing like that to such an inaccessible place, goodness only knows. And just how he moved his goods to the markets, I found it hard to imagine. The ranch was thirty miles of the most brutal terrain imaginable from the nearest settlement at Superior, let alone anywhere else. You have to hand it to the mad old hermit, he can't have been quite as daft as he looked.

After my pleasant coffee and porridge interlude at the Reavis Ranch, the day became rapidly tough and brutal. I had been really looking forward to seeing the Eastern Superstitions but the trail all day was truly awful; what looked on the map to be a comfortable and well defined trail was in reality an incessant series of 500ft climbs and descents on steep, horribly stony and frequently overgrown trails. Most of the day I crawled along covering about three miles every two hours, always watching my feet on the sharp and loose rocks that passed for a trail. Spiky bushes crowded in around my legs and I was glad to be wearing long trousers which afforded some measure of protection.

The scenery was fantastic with wonderful sharp peaks and canyons appearing round every corner but I was too irritated with the trail to enjoy the day much. Somewhat uncharitably I thought that for a part of the Arizona Trail that was so close to the Phoenix area, it should have been better kept. Chris Townsend had found much of this section to be overgrown when he walked it in 2001 and not much seemed to have been done to improve matters since.

Late in the afternoon, the going became substantially better after I crossed Two Bar Ridge. The sparkling blue of Roosevelt Lake appeared ahead for the first time and there were distant views of tomorrow's challenge, the Four Peaks, and the massive bulk of the Mazatzals beyond. The dreadful rocky, overgrown paths had given way to a stony jeep track and I made good enough progress to reach Cottonwood Creek that evening. Although windy, Cottonwood Creek had plenty of water and was within spitting distance of Roosevelt Lake where I had high hopes of a good breakfast and somewhere to replenish my dwindling food stores.

Day 18, Cottonwood Creek to Granite Spring, 15 miles

What a massive disappointment Roosevelt Lake proved to be! I got going at a quarter past seven on a cloudy and cool morning looking forward to an early stop and a huge breakfast at what the trail notes promisingly described as "Grocery Store and Café".

When I reached the lake shore just before 9 o'clock a chilly wind was whipping across the grey water and the place looked totally deserted, altogether not quite the inviting azure lake I had seen from the top of the Superstitions the previous afternoon. However I headed straight for the huge and lavish looking Tonto Ranger Centre, half a mile back from the marina, hoping to pick up some expert information on weather and trail conditions and on water sources up ahead in the Four Peaks Wilderness and the Mazatzals.

I found two charming looking elderly ladies smartly dressed in their Ranger khakis so I explained what I was doing and asked if they knew the latest forecast before I headed off into the mountains. "No, not really. Might get a bit warmer tomorrow, maybe".

"What about up north beyond Pine? Has there been much snow?" I persisted. "Oh, I wouldn't know about that either".

I decided not to try them with an issue as taxing as asking about water sources up ahead and so tried something simpler, "Do you know where I can get some food around here?"

"Nowhere for ten miles", they replied.

"But I thought there was a grocery store or café at Roosevelt Lake".

"Oh, there's one of those down at the marina".

This was not quite the level of expertise I might have expected from the US Ranger Service but I thanked them for their help and without much confidence I trotted off across two huge empty car parks and along a 600 yard pontoon to the sizeable marina, full of boats but totally devoid of people. There I found a tiny, ill-stocked store and, in a land where service is almost universally superb, possibly America's most unhelpful assistant.

Despite the fact that I was probably her first and perhaps only customer of the morning, the girl offered me no help whatsoever as I struggled to find the things I needed in the store, staying firmly rooted to her seat and a bag of Doritos. I asked if there was any hot food available and she replied "There's burgers in the freezer".

Five minutes of rooting around in the freezer and I had drawn a complete blank on the burger front. By now I had completely lost it, "Look, you're going to have to help me here. I've just come off two weeks on the Arizona Trail, I'm tired and hungry and I can't find the burgers you say are in the freezer". The girl shrugged, reluctantly got off her stool and wandered over to peer unenthusiastically into the freezer "We haven't got any, that's why", before returning to her stool and Doritos.

With copious quantities of steam coming out of my ears I heated up a couple of dismal looking frozen hot dogs, made myself some coffee and took the hot dogs, the coffee, my pack and my shopping outside in four separate journeys as my new best friend stayed rooted to her seat and sullenly watched me struggle with the swing door.

If my mood was sour at that point, it was about to get a whole lot worse. My new Walmart boots, which by now had all of 50 miles on the clock, had been feeling a bit lumpy on the way down to the lake and so I took them off to find out if there was something stuck in them. To my horror, both boots had huge cracks across the heels and each heel had moved outwards by a good half inch. They had the appearance of boots that someone with an odd gait might have been wearing for say, five years. I seriously doubted if they would make it much further.

Looking at the map I could see that Payson, 45 miles up the road, might be my best bet and so I decided to see if I could hitch there. But by early afternoon I was still walking up and down an almost deserted Highway 188 after two fruitless hours of waving my thumb and smiling hopefully at the few passing motorists. The only people who stopped were a group of Canadian bikers who wanted me to take a picture of them. I gave up and decided to give the mountains a go and see if I could get to Pine, around ninety miles away by the trail, before the boots completely gave out. If I stuck as much as possible to the dirt tracks known as Forest Roads, I would do better than on the hard rocky trails but my maps showed me that most of the way that would not be an option.

A track led away from the lake and up Vineyard Canyon to bring me back to the Arizona Trail a few miles along, just where the climb up to Lone Pine Saddle really gets itself nicely warmed up. The Four Peaks is by no means the highest or biggest climb on the trail but it rises steeply from Roosevelt Lake at around 2000ft to top out between Buckhorn Mountain and Lone Pine Saddle at almost 6000ft. Climbing up to Buckhorn involves an energy sapping five mile climb rising very sharply for 2500ft. And despite the best efforts of the Arizona Trail Association to clear away vegetation and fire damage, that section is notoriously difficult to get through, sometimes appearing to plunge into deep undergrowth whilst at other times the shrubbery had been cleared away for several feet either side.

My mood remained grim. On top of an overriding feeling of weariness, my brush with civilization at Roosevelt Lake had been almost laughably bad, the surprise discovery that my boots were falling apart, two hours by the side of the 188 and now this climb. Instead of enjoying the mighty views back to the lake and to the Mazatzals ahead, I could only see it as something to get through. The only good thing about the day was that it was surprisingly cool and windy. Goodness only knows how I would have coped with that climb in the heat of two or three days before – I wonder if I might just have chucked in the towel and headed to Phoenix and the next plane home.

I made camp a few miles from Lone Pine Saddle but much higher up than I would have liked. It was over 5500ft up and with nothing much to stop the chill breeze I put my tent down on the floor of a dusty hollow which gave some measure of shelter from the north westerly wind. Tomorrow, I hoped, would be a better day.

Day 19, Four Peaks to near Sunflower, 23 miles

Tomorrow was not a better day. In fact it was by far my worst day on the Arizona Trail and brought me within a whisker of quitting. The day started well enough with the fabulous sight of Roosevelt Lake shimmering way below in the early morning sunlight. Whatever you might feel about a man-made lake in the middle of the wilderness, it was a thing of great beauty just at that moment and, without dams and man-made lakes, the population of most of Arizona would not be able to make their home in the state.

The track down from the Lone Pine Saddle Trailhead was a good one and should have lifted my mood. For ten miles I meandered along on a wide, flat, well surfaced forest road through lovely high pine woods but as the morning wore on, my thoughts became increasingly negative. My body was protesting noisily; limping along on the side of my rapidly disintegrating boots, any part of me which had been injured in recent years was starting to flare up – my right knee, my Achilles tendon that had been giving me grief just before leaving England and now my back was protesting. In addition several deep blisters had appeared on both feet, all this caused by walking in poor boots for just a couple of days.

I spent much of the day wondering what on earth I was doing there, far away from friends and family, wandering around the wilderness, bearded, wild-haired and filthy. Sometimes a plane from Phoenix would rumble overhead and more than once I wished that I was on it, heading back to all the luxuries of home life – comfort, cleanliness, warm beds, good food, even television!

Then, to cap it all, I made a major route finding error. I knew that for the last eight miles into the tiny settlement of Sunflower, the trail took an obscure and difficult path northwest along Boulder Creek Canyon and I also knew exactly where the turn off should be. But, despite looking out for the left turn marker, I simply couldn't see it. I wandered on hopefully for at least a mile then turned around, retraced my steps and walked past it again and back up the trail for another mile. And then back again. The turn-off had apparently ceased to exist.

Finally, fully two hours after I had first passed it, I spotted a little trail marker on the opposite side of the road to where I had been looking, on the east side of the trail for a track that was heading west. It did little to improve my glum mood although I was greatly relieved to have finally found the way down to Sunflower.

The path down Boulder Creek was as bad as any of the overgrown, rocky trails I had found in the Superstitions. In 2002 Chris Townsend had written "The first part of the descent was rough, rocky and very overgrown. The vegetation clung and stuck and tore, as usual." Ten years later and the trail was no better but I was grateful I was still wearing my long trousers, as I had been all through the Superstitions and Four Peaks, instead of the shorts I might have preferred in the afternoon heat. For several miles I followed a narrow and rocky streambed until it finally opened out into a grassy, ranching area where cattle trails criss-crossed each other and constantly led me off in the wrong direction.

Utterly exhausted, I made camp in amongst the cattle tracks as soon as I found a flat piece of ground. Gloomily I prodded all the bits of my body that hurt and examined my boots. They had completely given up the ghost – both heels now had huge holes in them, big enough to put my thumbs through. They were completely unusable.

In a strange way I was almost glad to have made that discovery. Now I had no choice about trying to get up into the Mazatzals and along the Ridgeline. I would have to find some way of getting to Payson where I felt sure I would be able to buy some decent replacements. Then I could make my way to Pine and regroup for the second half of the journey.

Day 20, Sunflower to Payson to LF Ranch, 23 miles walking, 30 in a car

Yesterday's disasters carried on into the night when a howling wind got up and blew my tent over, twice, tearing off one of the main guy rope attachments in the process which left part of the front of my tent flapping haplessly in the wind. Running repairs would be needed at Pine but that episode confirmed my earlier thoughts about using the tent as a giant groundsheet and sleeping in the open. It certainly made for more peaceful nights instead of always worrying about it blowing down around my ears and I really enjoyed just lying there looking at the moon and stars. Somehow I felt much more at one with nature. I didn't feel any colder sleeping out.

I walked the remaining five miles to Sunflower not quite sure just what I would find there, but the trail notes were not too encouraging, suggesting that not even water was amongst its scant attractions. In fact the seductively named settlement made my little Norfolk village of Thursford Green look as exciting as Las Vegas. It consisted of four small houses and some kind of construction company with Highway 87 slicing straight through the middle. Clearly not the place to find a taxi to Payson.

So I plonked myself by the side of the 87 and stuck my thumb out with little hope of any success after the previous day's dismal failure at Roosevelt Lake. But lo and behold, within a couple of minutes a clapped out old coupe screeched to a smoky halt right by me.

It turned out that Andy, a housekeeper of some kind at the Diamond Resorts' Kohl Ranch Lodge, had spotted me and decided to do his good deed for the day. If he hadn't been clocking 90mph between police checkpoints, I could have hugged him. Not only would he drop me in Payson but he knew exactly where I could get a pair of boots and he would take me right there. Andy dropped me outside a small shop called "Hike, Bike and Run" which turned out to be a veritable Tardis of everything that you might need to, yes, you've guessed it, hike, bike and run.

I happily parted with $114 for an excellent pair of Merrells, my third pair of boots in six days and hopefully my last of the trip. After Pine I would head up on to the 7000ft high plateau beyond the Mogollon Rim where the going should be much less rocky and therefore softer on the feet and less ruinous to my boots.

I asked the little shop to give my five day old boots a decent burial and, with a distinct spring in my step, trotted across the road to a café for perhaps the most delicious and welcome breakfast I have ever eaten. Eggs, bacon and pancakes lavishly covered in maple syrup, all washed down with three cups of coffee.

BREAKFASTS AND OTHER CULINARY DELIGHTS

My trail diet of noodles, porridge and trail bars was pretty dull and monotonous, suitable really only to sustain life rather than to delight the senses. I was hungry much of the time and so when I reached any kind of settlement, whatever I ate would taste like the most delicious thing I had ever eaten.

Each and every meal I ate outside of my campsites was a real joy. It made me realise that we often just throw food down our

---

necks without really savouring it in any way and so to find myself enjoying every mouthful of even the simplest dish was a great treat.

Breakfasts were particularly superb and I quickly grew to relish the American breakfast of eggs, bacon, pancakes and maple syrup*, although I was never brave enough to order one of the "Big Stack" options. Even in my famished condition a heap of five or six pancakes would have defeated me. Breakfast was always accompanied by as many refills of coffee as you could drink before starting to shake uncontrollably, usually at least three big mugs in my case. There would always be an interesting collection of creams to go with the coffee – hazelnut and mocha, I remember with particular affection.

Dinners always tasted fantastic. I mostly dined in Mexican restaurants or bars where burgers and beer would feature strongly. The luxury of some beers to go with my supper was a huge treat, although after several dry days on the trail I had to watch my consumption. More than once a couple of glasses would have me wobbling when I stepped down from my bar stool.

Everywhere I went the service was genuinely friendly and always quick and efficient and if I was sitting at the bar I would almost invariably strike up conversations with complete strangers who seemed genuinely interested in what I was doing.

* I was so taken with the American breakfast that I now serve that as an option at Holly Lodge.

Poring over my maps with the aid of a third cup of coffee to get my brain kick-started, I had to make a quick decision on what to do next. There seemed to be three options. The least attractive one was to try to get back to Sunflower but with no guarantee of another Andy coming to my rescue, that was no certainty. Besides, breaking in new boots with a pair of very sore feet inside them across the entire length of the Mazatzals might not be my best career move.

Or I could just walk fifteen miles straight up Highway 87 and reach Pine that evening, which seemed quite an attractive idea but a bit of a cop out.

In the end I went for a good old British compromise and opted to take a 16 mile forest road that would put me back on the Arizona Trail towards the end of the mountains and around 25 miles from Pine. The Mazatzals would have to wait for another time but I felt greatly pleased with the decision, my improved mood and most of all, my comfy new boots. In less than half a day I had gone from being within an inch of going home to finding a way to carry on to Pine.

The track out of Payson, Forest Road 406, was a delight, as were the town's historic buildings that lined the road for the first mile or so. I was much taken with Payson and decided that it was a place I would like to come back to one day for a better look. For a dozen miles I strode out along a well kept dirt track, able to walk properly for the first time in several days as I enjoyed the comfort of my new Merrells. There was little to grab my attention, apart from the approaching bulk of the Mazatzals ahead and to my left, but it was a

Up in the Matazals

lovely warm afternoon and I felt in much better spirits again.

Late in the afternoon I passed the curiously named Doll Baby Ranch (a sad story involving the early death of the rancher's baby daughter in 1902) and then the broad sweep of the East Verde River where I would find the Arizona Trail again. Not long afterwards I passed the LV Ranch and found what would surely be one of my prettiest campsites of the entire trail, right by the slow flowing waters of the East Verde. Little did I know what I had let myself in for.

RANCHES

Despite much of the trail being in remote wilderness areas, signs of cattle would be my constant companion throughout Arizona. But ranching was clearly quite a different thing to our British model where a hundred or more cows can be grazed in a nice green grassy field the size of a couple of football pitches, only to be moved on to the next one when they have had their fill of lush grass.

In Arizona cattle are spread out over vast areas, so vast that if I ever actually saw a cow it would be a big surprise. Just what the cattle found to eat out there I have no idea but the few that I did see looked astonishingly well fed. All along the trail was evidence that you were in cattle country – fences, gates, stockades, cattle tanks and very, very occasionally a remote property called a ranch. But so subtle were these signs that they never really interfered with the natural landscape. In any case I would often be sincerely grateful for a cattle tank or trough, however murky, to fill my water bottles from.

The only thing that I took issue with were the many, many gates I passed through on the trail. Each one seemed to be of a completely unique design, necessitating a certain amount of ingenuity to open and close it successfully. Worst of all were what are known as cowboy gates, big, wide makeshift arrangements usually kept closed with very tightly strung barbed wire which was often almost impossible to deal with. Sometimes I just gave up, threw my pack over and climbed over them.

Day 21, LF Ranch to Oak Springs, 20 miles

The Mazatzal Wilderness covers a massive 250,000 acres and yet I managed to pick the only noisy place in the entire area. How was I to know that my idyllic campsite by the green waters of the East Verde River was also, unbeknown to me, just the other side of some trees from the LV Ranch?

I only realised that when I heard several dogs going completely berserk, quite possibly disturbed by my presence just the other side of their fence. A woman yelled "Shad erp!" which they did and I thought that would be the end of it for the night. Then at 7.30 the world's loudest generator cranked into action with a great rumbling noise like a passenger jet getting ready to take off.

The trouble is, once you have pitched camp and it has gone dark, which was happening around 6.30pm, it is too late to move. Since you can't see anything beyond the reach of a small head torch it is just not possible to pick everything up and move on. I was stuck there until dawn, just as I had been with the freight trains near Cienega Creek.

Still, I imagined that these good country folk would be hitting the sack around 9 o'clock leaving me in blissful peace. But not a bit of it – it was midnight before the blasted thing finally stopped rumbling away. Four hours later their cockerels kicked off, presumably under the misapprehension that it was dawn, which it wasn't and wouldn't be for another 2½ hours.

After my poor night's sleep the day's walking was all a bit ho hum. With just 24 miles to Pine I might have pressed on and reached the town by the evening but as far as I could see there was only one place to stay and my British B&B experience told me that turning up late on a Saturday evening without booking in advance might be foolish. So I throttled back and finished a relatively comfortable day four miles short of Pine.

As it turned out the going was much tougher than the "easy to moderate" suggested by the trail notes. There were several long, rocky climbs to flat topped mesas. On top of that some very indistinct trails made for tricky route finding. As I crested Polles Mesa, Whiterock Mesa and Saddle Ridge I felt quite chuffed with myself for not losing the trail all day. But all morning I had to stop and check where the next cairn was and, as had been the way with most of the Arizona Trail, it was always very, very stony underfoot.

To celebrate not getting lost, and because I had plenty of time in hand, I took my pack off, stripped off my shirt and had a snooze in the sun, the one and only time I would afford myself such a luxury the whole way. Just beyond the Mazatzal Wilderness boundary, the aptly named Hardscrabble Mesa led down towards Pine. It was too steep to camp on and I found myself near the bottom at the very pleasant Oak Spring before I found a spot flat enough to pitch camp. Next day I would be able to breakfast early in Pine and would have two full days to regroup. It was a most enticing prospect.

No need for a tent tonight

Chapter 9

PINE INTERLUDE

"When people have chosen a certain path, they should walk it with satisfaction."
Aung San Suu Kyi

RESUPPLY TOWN ROUTINE

Nothing ever worked out completely perfectly in the little towns dotted on or near the Arizona Trail which served as resupply towns, usually because of the huge area of land that even the smallest Arizona settlement occupies or because some of the places I needed were closed, often because I had the uncanny knack of arriving in towns at weekends. But in an ideal world, this is how things should have happened in a resupply town.

I would hope to go straight to the US Post Office to collect my post box, check in at a motel, take a shower, put on my town clothes from the post box and stick my filthy trail clothes in the motel's washing machines – almost every motel in America miraculously seems to have a room with a huge washing machine and tumble drier and powder available in small containers, all at a fraction of the price you would pay in a British launderette.

Then I would go off and get something to eat, find the town library from where I could send some e-mails and check out any information I needed about the trail ahead, then visit

---

whatever passed for a supermarket to stock up on food for the next few days. The rest of the time would be spent sorting out my kit, charging up camera batteries and Kindle, eating again and finally repacking my post box to send on to the next town. All that was an awful lot of personal admin to get through in just a few hours and left me with precious little time for the thing I needed most, namely rest.

In practice the routine only worked out like that in Patagonia. At Oracle I was thrown off course by the town's motel being unmanned for three hours, at Superior and now at Pine I had arrived at a weekend when libraries and Post Offices were closed. I would also arrive in Flagstaff at a weekend.

Hunger got the better of me when I reached Pine and so I went straight into Early Birds, a peculiarly American type of diner specialising in serving gargantuan breakfasts and open only between 6am and 2 pm. Our nearest British equivalent is the working men's café, most of which are rapidly disappearing from our streets in favour of chain coffee shops with names like Costalot and Bigbucks.

It was packed out at 9 o'clock on a Sunday morning which told me firstly that it must be very good and secondly that going out to Sunday breakfast was clearly a popular pastime in the States. It certainly was good, so good in fact that I went back there on subsequent days for two more breakfasts and a lunch, although I never again attempted anything as stomach stretching as my breakfast that first morning of two eggs, hash browns, corned beef hash and a pancake the size of a Frisbee. I sat contentedly at the bar for almost two lazy hours and chatted to Geoff, a Pine resident who had moved there from Phoenix but was finding it hard going trying to sell real estate in a depressed market.

Finally it was time to tear myself away and head to my first choice of accommodation, the excellent looking but totally deserted Pine Creek Cabins. I asked at the Nifty 50s Diner next door. "She's probably in church", said the diner's owner somewhat disparagingly. Butch, a good ol' boy with a beard like Father Christmas, let me use his phone to ring up our good Christian lady but there was no reply.

I tried Butch's phone again a while later and hung around until after one o'clock before giving up and gloomily heading back a mile down the road to the not quite so promising looking Rimside Grill and Cabins, a motel that I had passed by four hours earlier. In fact by default I had made an excellent choice. I got a great welcome and a lovely little cabin for only $32.50, their special rate for Arizona Trail hikers. So far on the journey I had been charged anywhere between $32.50 and $67 for roughly similar rooms in similar towns, which was odd but still dirt cheap by British standards.

The afternoon was spent gloriously loafing about in the sun outside my cabin before trekking back up the road into what passed for the centre of Pine for a wander about and to check out the resupply options at the Ponderosa Market. As had been the case at Oracle it was not a market at all but a perfectly nice small supermarket. It had everything I needed for the trail ahead, including a cheap pair of gloves for the cold mornings ahead, somewhat thicker than the lightweight ones I had optimistically brought with me.

The real bonus at the Rimside was that I had probably my best meal of the entire trip in their restaurant and some superb beer from their own microbrewery. In fact I would drink microbrewery beer for the remainder of the trip since every place I visited subsequently was supplied by the amazing Beaver Street Brewery in Flagstaff, a hostelry at which I would spend three happy, if slightly fuzzy evenings the following week.

Beer in America is often light years away from the brown coloured alcoholic water sold by industrial companies such as Budweiser and Miller. All over the States are microbreweries producing wonderfully flavoursome and often quite strong brews and if you look hard you will find some of these beers in the supermarkets there as well. Americans have absolutely no excuse for drinking the stuff that most of them do but perhaps we in Britain should not laugh too much at American beer drinking habits. After all, a country that drank things like Worthington E and Watneys Red Barrel through much of the 60s and 70s and then moved on to some pretty dull tasting lagers should perhaps come down off its high horse when it comes to American beer.

I was much taken by something I read on the menu of the Rimside Bar and Grill which read:-
"If you always do what you've always done
You'll always be where you've always been".
As with many great little quotes, it turns out that nobody famous ever actually said that but Henry Ford said something very similar and so generally gets the credit for the quote. Thinking about that, if somebody like me came up with something quotable, no matter how witty it was, and the chances are it probably wouldn't be that witty, nobody would ever quote it. Then at the other end of the quotability scale were people like Oscar Wilde or Winston Churchill who must have had a little man following them around with a notebook and pencil writing down everything they said, just so that the rest of London could quote it hilariously the very next day.

Day 23, Pine to Pine, No miles just up and down Highway 87 three times.

After three weeks on the trail without a rest day, my day off in Pine was just what I needed to recharge my batteries, both the literal and metaphorical kind. The last few miles into town had been a real effort and when I sat down on my stool at the Early Bird Diner, I was all done in.

Monday was not a total rest day but it gave me a great chance to take stock, think about what I had done so far and to get myself ready for the rest of the trail. Needless to say, all ideas of a good lie-in went out of the window when I woke up at my usual tent time of six o'clock, partly because I was now firmly in the habit of waking up at six but mostly because I was freezing cold. I hadn't yet fathomed out how to stop the heater in my cabin making an irritating blowing noise and so had switched it off the previous evening. I would better understand the complexities of the heating later but something quite different and unexpected would disturb my second night in the cabin, more of which anon.

So it was off to the Early Bird Diner for another slap-up breakfast and then back up the road to pick up my post box when the Post Office opened its doors at eight o'clock. Once again I was charmed by the small town friendliness of the place and as ever, surprised and gratified to find that the parcel I had sent to myself had actually arrived.

The rest of the morning was spent on a good old prolonged kit faff – sorting though all my things, doing some running repairs to the tent with the aid of some glue and an office stapler borrowed from the motel and shuffling trail notes and maps for the rest of the walk.

TAKING STOCK

Encouragingly I was now well over half way to Utah. I had already come 460 miles from the Mexican Border in just 22 days of walking. That left not much more than 340 miles to go with an absolute maximum of 19 days left. Even allowing for a bit of mucking around with the notoriously erratic permit system at the Grand Canyon, unless anything else went very wrong, finishing the trail and finishing on time looked quite possible.

Physically I had walked myself into the ground by cracking on to Pine so quickly but just as long as I didn't get ill or over-exhausted from lack of sustenance, I had clearly found my "trail legs" and should be able to cover some good daily mileages on the flat ground to come. My sore feet were healing up nicely and the new boots had been a great success.

The worst terrain was now over. Apart from the odd aberration like the climb out of Pine up and over the Mogollon Rim the next day and the exciting trip through the Grand Canyon, the rest of the route was across a flattish 7000ft high plateau with plenty of dirt tracks and much less rock.

So far the Arizona Trail had been much, much tougher than I had expected. Perhaps I had been fooled by the pristine nature of English long distance paths like the South Downs Way or even my local Norfolk Coastal Path. On those the way is easy to see and the going underfoot clear of stones, rocks and general debris.

Perhaps I had expected a bit more from a trail that wants to put itself right up there with the big American "must-do" trails like the Appalachian or the Pacific Crest. I shouldn't have been surprised by the mountains, after all, they are there on the map for all to see but, my goodness, they just keep on coming and with some ferocity.

What had surprised me most was just how hard some of the trail was underfoot – two ruined pairs of boots in 460 miles was a testament to that. But I suppose that is just good old Arizona Rock; hard, unforgiving and tough to shift out of the way to please a soft-booted British hiker.

I had also been dismayed by just how many sections were overgrown with tough, spiky bushes growing in across the trail from both sides. Maybe the vegetation grows fast in the mountains but some areas, particularly in the Superstitions and near Sunflower looked as if they had not been cut back for several years. More often than I had expected, I had to wear long trousers to protect my legs from being shredded.

I probably also hadn't expected route finding to be so difficult with long passages being so indistinct that I constantly needed to stop and look around for the next sign of a trail ahead. So far I had only lost the path three or four times but it had often needed a huge exercise in concentration.

If that all sounds unduly harsh, it is not meant to be. Up to Pine I had been thrilled with all sorts of things – the scenery, the weather (during the day, if not at night), the detailed Arizona

Trail notes, the wonderful people I had met, the resupply towns, the reasonable availability of water even in the most arid landscapes. Most of all perhaps, and please pass me my trumpet, I was more than a little thrilled with myself for managing to get that far without a total catastrophe and to be able to survive out in the wilderness for three weeks. I now looked forward to meeting a whole different set of challenges on the rest of the journey. For a total novice it was a huge step up from the fear with which I had approached the start of the trail.

Pine was proving to be a great little rejuvenator and I was glad that I had chosen to spend my two day stop there rather than at Superior. It was a terrific feeling to have come more than half way and to have put most of the big climbs behind me. But most of all, Pine was just a fine place to spend a couple of days whether I was recuperating or not.

Dotted around several hillsides, Pine and its sister town Strawberry, just two miles up Highway 87, are both at more than 5000ft above sea level. The properties are very spread out and most are built to look like Alpine chalets. The attractive houses and the high altitude have turned the area into a great summer escape for the people the locals slightly scathingly call "Flatlanders", those from Phoenix and the flat valley around the burgeoning city who come to enjoy temperatures typically 30F below those of Phoenix. That would be very seductive when the valley temperature climbs to 100F or more, which it does for most of the summer.

The only problem with being a summer escape is that more than half the houses are deserted for the better part of the year which rather takes the stuffing out of the community. Property prices spiral for locals who can't afford to fork out the high prices that are easily affordable by the more affluent Flatlanders. It all sounded a very familiar tale, not unlike the problems caused by second home ownership in my home area of North Norfolk.

That evening, the Rimside Grill's excellent restaurant was closed so I thought I would try my luck at Sidewinders, a well known bar in the centre of town. It was all that I could have asked for – good beers, excellent food and a cast of interesting locals, many with ZZ Top style beards, none of whom seemed to resent the presence of the English stranger in their bar.

I chatted at some length to the owner, Tony Gianndrea, a grey haired man of around sixty endowed with an enormous, quiet charisma. Clearly everyone knew him and looked immensely pleased to see him – there was a great deal of handshaking going on when he entered the bar. He never really told me what had brought him to Pine ten years before but he had clearly found his niche in life with Sidewinders.

At 6.30 the bar cleared as the entire crowd moved away to a side area to play Texas Hold'em, a form of poker. I suppose it was the American equivalent of our pub quiz nights. I ate my meal in peace, reluctantly decided against another beer and headed back up Highway 87 for an early night.

Initially sleep proved disappointingly elusive, as it often did when I was in a real bed, but I had just nodded off around about eleven o'clock when I was treated to a bizarre visit from the local sheriff's boys in brown. From somewhere back in Row 47 my sleepy brain registered an insistent banging noise, repeated a few seconds later, slightly louder. I ignored it thinking it must be coming from the cabin next door, if I was capable of thinking at all in my befuddled state.

Next time the banging was really loud and so I shot out of bed, hastily threw some trousers on and went to the door, more than a little nervously, it has to be said. Surrounding my cabin doorway were no less than three brown uniformed sheriffs, deputies or whatever. They said that there had been reports of a fight going on nearby and asked me if I had heard anything. I mumbled that I hadn't heard anything at all; they apologised for disturbing me and cleared off. It was all very strange. Needless to say it took me a very long time to get back to sleep after that.

Chapter 10

PLODDING ACROSS THE PLATEAU

PINE TO FLAGSTAFF, 120 miles

*"I wanted a little of that swagger that comes with being able to
gaze at a far horizon through eyes of chipped granite and say with
a slow, manly sniff, "Yeah, I've shit in the woods""*
Bill Bryson, A Walk in the Woods

Day 24, Pine to the Mogollon Rim, 23 miles

I couldn't leave Pine without another Early Bird breakfast to sustain
me for the day ahead. As I ate my bacon, eggs and pancakes with
rather more maple syrup than was strictly necessary, even for
someone intending to walk more than 20 miles with a fully loaded
pack, I had much to ponder.

Pine was the stepping off point for the second phase of the Arizona
Trail, the high plateau, a land of forests, lakes and high altitude. I
had well and truly left the desert behind and would be unlikely to
see another cactus until the Utah border, where desert vegetation
starts all over again. Blocking my path to the Colorado Plateau lay
the Mogollon Rim, an unbroken green line on the map snaking its
way from east to west but on the ground a dark and threatening cliff
visible from almost anywhere in Pine. It had been uppermost in my
mind throughout my time in the little town; more than one person
had issued me with warnings about just how steep the trail up the
Mogollon Rim might be and a fire fighter I spoke to thought it might
be in poor condition, possibly impassable.

114

So I set off along the clearly marked Highline Trail which led eastward out of town with a certain amount of nervousness about just what the day might bring. The Highline Trail was lovely – a historic trail dating from the 19th Century when ranchers used it to visit each other's homesteads, just what I needed to get going again; sound earth underfoot and gently undulating through glorious pine woods laced with ample streams. If I could have walked all the way to Utah on such a trail, I would have been a very happy camper.

A couple of times I ran into day hikers, a rare sight up to now on the Arizona trail but mostly I enjoyed the quiet of the woods undisturbed. I enjoyed too a new spring in my step, partly generated by a couple of days rest and partly by the softer, more forgiving underfoot conditions. But the Mogollon Rim grew ever closer and I wondered what that might bring.

I needn't have worried. The naysayers, I rather fancied, had probably never climbed up the trail to the top. Although it was indeed a tortuous and steep climb of around 2000ft, the trail was perfectly passable and far from dangerous. If I stopped and looked back there were some fine views of the distant Mazatzals and at one point I had a reminder of my generator disturbed night by the East Verde River. A stream that crashed down the cliff near the trail was apparently the beginnings of the selfsame river.

My view of the Mazatzals would be my last chance for a long look back down the trail. From now on the horizon would be much more limited and I would no longer be able to see where I might be in a few days' time or where I had been a week ago. I was entering a very different landscsape.

Cresting the Rim past an area of fire damage I took one last look back and headed north into the trees. Just a few hundred yards back from the top I walked straight into something that I had not been prepared for at all, great banks of snow lying everywhere.

Everyone I had spoken to had told me what a dry winter it had been in Arizona with weather fronts moving round the outside of the state leaving the land bone dry and there was the threat of forest fires and

▲ *First sight of snow on the Mogollon Rim*

▼ *Fire damage on the Rim*

water shortages later in the year. But up there at 7000ft there was a great deal of snow, quite probably from earlier in the winter, and most of it was lying exactly where I wanted to walk.

I had hoped to camp near General Springs Cabin, which was not named after a General Springs at all but a General Crook, who led the US Army in the Indian wars of the 1870s. The story goes that he used a spring near the restored cabin whilst passing through the area, hence the name of the cabin. It was probably one of the least noteworthy historical stories I had ever come across.

I never did find the esteemed general's cabin. The Arizona Trail soon became completely impossible to follow in the deep snow and I had to do a quick sidestep via a couple of sporadically clear forest roads to make any further progress north. I managed to get about four miles away from the Rim before finding a lovely, snowless campsite right in the middle of some immensely tall pines. I put my tent down close by a huge fallen trunk which afforded some shelter from the sneaky wind and also made a pleasant seat for the evening's eating, smoking, writing and reading.

That night I pondered on a couple of intangibles. First of all, I wondered about the snow. How far north would it extend or would it be quite localised? In the few miles I had put in since cresting the Mogollon Rim I had made somewhat ponderous progress, to say the least. A couple of times I had sunk up to my hips in the white stuff and I was not particularly enjoying the sensation of soggy feet since neither my boots nor my socks were remotely waterproof.

The other intangible was just how cold it might get at night. Most nights so far had seen temperatures drop well below freezing point, even at some of the lower altitudes. The best I could hope for in the next three weeks would be night time values in the low 20s. By now I was rather regretting my carefully calculated decision to bring a lighter weight sleeping bag than I needed in these conditions so most nights I slept with practically every item of clothing on that I could find in my pack.

One thing that was not intangible was that I was most unlikely to come across the fabled Mogollon Monster. If you Google "Mogollon Monster" you will find a whole host of crackpot nonsense including several You Tube contributions, some of which are clearly just footage of somebody's mate loping through the woods dressed in a gorilla suit.

Yet reading a local paper in Pine I had come across a news item telling of how "Hundreds of people filled a haunted saloon to over-flowing on Thursday night to listen to a parade of Rim Country residents describe close encounters of the Bigfoot kind. Nineteen people recounted sightings of the Mogollon Monster described in various accounts as a 6 to 8 foot tall, shaggy, upright-walking creature with a pungent odour". Well, that would be me a few days out of Pine!

Day 25, Mogollon Rim to FR93, 22 miles

My big luck as I reached the high country was that Arizona was having a week of unseasonably warm weather. The Flatlanders of Phoenix were already sweltering in temperatures in the mid 90s whilst I would enjoy at least a couple of days in the 70s instead of the usual March highs for that altitude which usually hover in the low 50s.

WEATHER

You can pretty much divide Arizona's February and March climate into two. The southern bit, all those deserts and mountains that I had just crossed, should have a daytime high of between 55F and 75F, depending on how high up you are, with night time lows at least 30F lower. Rainfall is low and the sun shines about 90% of the time, which makes everyone in the southern half very happy, at least until the summer when people in the Phoenix Valley either stay near their air-conditioning or fry.

On the high plateau that stretches from the Mogollon Rim to Utah, winters are almost always cold and snowy. Usually things

---

have not perked up much by mid-March with daytime highs in the low 50s and night time lows in the high teens. It also frequently dumps snow by the bucket load in February and March, particularly around Flagstaff and on the North Rim of the Grand Canyon. That was why several locals had cautioned me against starting so early, but those who know me will confirm that the more people tell me something can't be done, the more I want to give it a go. No, it's not brave; it is just plain old stubbornness. A friend once told me that he only knew one person more stubborn than me and that was my father.

My first night on the plateau saw a low of 28F which was positively balmy compared to some of the nights I had struggled through so far and the daytime high was 68F, which was delightful. Long may it continue, I felt, although when I had watched the TV weather forecast just before leaving my cabin in Pine, the over-excited forecaster was getting himself quite overwrought about colder, wetter weather coming in at the weekend, which would probably mean snow in the notoriously cold Flagstaff area.

Despite the wonderful weather and the relatively flat terrain, my first full day on the Colorado Plateau became something of a trial, partly self-inflicted; in football commentator speak, a day of four halves. It all started so well, cracking along on some lovely forest roads, frozen firm from the night's frost and as flat as The Fens. My aim, if the trail was snow-free, was to romp along and reach Mormon Lake where there was a small settlement in just two days, fifty miles away.

The forest was lovely, mile after mile of high ponderosa pines, which was hardly surprising as I was now in the world's largest ponderosa pine forest. An interesting fact, I thought, but not that interesting perhaps unless you happen to be a connoisseur of ponderosa pine forests.

But then the trail dropped abruptly to the tongue twisting East Clear Creek. The descent was only 500ft but it was a north facing slope that had thawed and refrozen repeatedly and the further down I got, the trail became more and more icy. I was slipping around all over the place and fancied it less and less the further down I slid. Two thirds of the way to the bottom I rather timidly gave up and climbed back up to the top to try and find another way down and across the creek.

Soon I found myself in an area of steep sided canyons filled with dense, fallen, fire-damaged trees and it was there that I remembered the great Law of Forests. They are not that easy to find your way through. Out in the desert I had always had the next range of mountains or the sun to align myself with. In the forest, it was easy to find yourself going round in circles.

It took me two hours of increasingly frantic bushwhacking before I finally found another way down to the extremely pretty East Clear Creek and then a climb out the other side steeper than anything I had found in the mountains. Frankly by the end of it I rather wished I had been a bit less of a girl's blouse and had carried on with the original trail down to the floor of the canyon.

I soon rediscovered the Arizona Trail, ate a trail bar and drank some water from the creek and was ready for the third part of my day of four halves. Soon I found myself in an area of soft and very damp clay where for five or six tortuous miles the newly laid trail was more akin to walking across a ploughed field in winter. Heavy mud clung to my boots and hiking poles in great cloggy clumps. The not entirely pleasurable sensation of walking with diving boots on my feet was one that would become quite familiar in the days to come.

By mid-afternoon I had had enough and tried a clever little ruse to go round it all using a couple of tracks from the complex network of Forest Roads. Sadly the network proved to be too complex for my navigating skills and after heading inexorably back in the direction I had just come from, I needed to employ my second bit of strategic bushwhacking of the day before finding myself miraculously, and quite unexpectedly back on the Arizona Trail.

Late in the afternoon the trail eased substantially as I came into an area of sparse grassland and small trees, more like English parkland at the end of a hot summer. It was there that I saw the sight of the trail so far. From nowhere came a distant rumble like that of an approaching freight train – it signalled a huge herd of at least 200 elk crossing the open woodland just 100 yards in front of me. It was an awe-inspiring sight but I am afraid that I was too stupefied to whip out my camcorder fast enough to record the magnificent beasts. I did manage to snap off a few still photos but, as with most shots of moving animals, they were moving too fast and were too far away for the pictures to amount to much.

So far my wildlife sightings had been mostly of smaller animals, although I had seen quite a few white tailed deer along the way. I never did see a mule deer, a bighorn sheep or a pronghorn or any javelinas after the noisy herd I disturbed just outside Apache Junction, nor did I spot anything alarming like a bear or a mountain lion, though I did see some paw prints from one of the latter right next

Arizona's prettiest water source

to my tent one morning, which certainly made me think a bit. Bears and rattlesnakes should have still been hibernating that early in the year and, although I really, really do not like snakes at all, oddly I was slightly sad that I didn't see a snake of any kind all trip. (Ironically, two weeks after getting back to England I was out running on some North Norfolk heath land and very nearly trod on an adder basking in the spring sunshine). Coyotes were out on the plateau in numbers and I would frequently spy one eyeing me up from a distance – they didn't seem that bothered and would mostly ignore my presence and just go about their business.

Day 26, Forest Road 93 to almost Mormon Lake, 27 miles

After the coldest night on the trail so far with the temperature dropping to a teeth chattering 18F, I got away to an early start and made thumping good progress all day. I managed not to get lost once, despite endless complicated trail finding instructions and as a result, very nearly got to Mormon Lake that evening, thirty miles away.

As it turned out, I would have been mightily disappointed had I put in the extra three miles and arrived at Mormon Lake looking forward to a warm bed and cracking good meal. The Lodge was closed on a Thursday evening at that time of year and I would have found it shrouded in darkness.

Mormon Lake Lodge, by the way, had nothing whatsoever to do with Mormons apart from the fact that several Mormon families had a go at farming in the area in the 1870s before moving on to more promising lands. Nor, it has to be said, was Mormon Lake much of a lake but instead was a dried-up forty square mile mudflat which seldom holds much water for very long even in the wettest times.

Most of the day I walked through flat areas of open woodland interspersed with open yellow grasslands. Water was oddly scarce apart from that squelching beneath my feet on the stodgy trail which the Clerk of the Course at Fakenham Racecourse might have called "soft to very soft, good in places". All day, once the early morning frost had thawed, I walked with a ton of forest earth, leaves and pine needles stuck to my boots. Snow melting in the unseasonable heat had turned parts of the forest into a veritable swamp. Late in the afternoon and still three miles short of Mormon Lodge, I found a dry gully next to the track and settled in for the night.

HOME IS WHERE YOU PITCH IT

However much fun I might have been having wandering through the fabulous mountains, deserts and plateaux of the Arizona wilderness, the best part of the day was always the moment when I could stop walking, get the pack off my aching shoulders and make camp for the night. Food, contemplation of the day just passed and the challenges to come, reading and writing and finally blissful rest all made the nights in camp something I would look forward to all day.

It only took me an evening or two to establish what soon became an unshakeable routine. Towards the end of the afternoon, around 5.30 or 6 o'clock I would start looking for a good place to camp. It had to be flat and not too stony and, depending on the wind, as sheltered as possible. I would look for a flat gully or, in the forests, a large fallen tree trunk to shelter by. Water nearby was handy but not essential if I had enough in my water bottles and I became a bit fussy about finding somewhere with a nice big rock or a log where I could sit and eat, write and smoke.

Having found the ideal spot I would take everything out of my pack, taking great care not to put small things anywhere they might disappear into the undergrowth and sorting everything into four piles – cooking, tent, reading and writing, clothes and sundries.

First I would swap my trail clothes for camp clothes (no, not that sort of camp!) before the evening chill came down. Damp trail garments were hung on any convenient bush and I would then put on my Finisterre merino wool long johns and vest, a PHD lightweight down suit, fleece socks and down camp slippers. Not making me much of a fashion icon but my goodness, I was glad of each and every item all through the trip.

Next I would get a fire going, collecting twigs and small stuff to go in the bottom of my Ti-Tri Inferno. I have to admit that I never became an expert fire lighter and all too often the fire would burn out before I had got anything cooked, but mostly it worked well enough. Juniper burnt well, I found, and the added bonus was that it gave off a pleasant smell.

Whilst I was boiling up some water, I could put the tent up if I wanted, or just arrange it on the ground with my mat and sleeping bag on top, always taking care that there were no lumpy bits underneath. By the time the tent was done, my water would be boiling and I could make some food, never, sadly, any variation from the dried noodle or rice dishes available in the little supermarkets in the resupply towns.

Food eaten and cooking pot roughly cleaned I would settle down on my rock or log for a smoke and then write up the day's happenings in a Moleskine notebook. Another smoke and it would be time to retire to my tent for a good study of the maps and trail notes for the next day's walking and then, best of all, a good hour's reading before settling down for the night. I had brought a Kindle, which is perfect for a long trip. On it was a Stieg Larsson for easy reading, Bill Bryson's lengthy but amusing "At Home" and Henry Thoreau's slightly ponderous "Walking". I also picked up several second hand paperbacks in libraries along the way, mostly for the princely sum of 50 or 75 cents. That way I was introduced to John Grisham (excellent) and James Paterson (average but entertaining).

I also read for the third time Chris Townsend's Arizona Crossing, the account of his walk over exactly the same trail in 2002. Each night I read the appropriate passages for the next day's trail and it gave me a great idea of what to look out for, what kind of terrain was coming up, and the natural history I might see along the way. I loved his wry, matter-of-fact writing style and knew that I could never be half as good at observing and recognising the natural world.

Sleep was generally a fractured affair. Even the most hardened trail veteran will admit to not sleeping all that well lying on the ground. I suppose we are so used to our comfy mattresses that camping comes as a bit of a shock to the system. My night's sleep would be erratic, no particular pattern to when I might wake up in the middle of the night, or indeed how often; crawling out of the tent for a pee and back in before losing all my sleeping bag warmth. Sometimes I might not go back to sleep straight away and would lie there thinking about the next day's challenges. On the worst nights cold would get in the way of sleep.

Still, most nights I would get six or seven hours of reasonable sleep and wake with first light at around six o'clock. The sun usually crept over the horizon about 6.30 and if I had been really clever the night before, I would have made camp so as to take advantage of the sun's first rays. But usually it would be a while before they gave out much warmth and almost every morning of the journey I would be much colder than I wanted to be until I got a mile or two along the trail.

If I found an organised routine for making camp from the very first evening, I never really got into any sort of pattern for breaking camp in the morning. Some mornings I made a fire, ate some porridge and drank a coffee, others I just took a few sips of frozen water and then made breakfast an hour or so up the trail. Most days I was too sleepy, stiff and cold to be bothered much with anything besides filling all my stuff sacs, packing everything in to the rucksack and getting going without leaving half my kit behind. Before leaving camp I would always scour every inch of my campsite for any stray kit and I am pleased to say that the routine worked a treat – after losing three separate items of kit before I even set out on day one, I made it to the very last day without shedding a single item of gear.

I wish I could present you with a picture of yours truly sitting on a rock, steaming mug of coffee in hand breathing in the fresh morning air and watching the first rays of the sun creep over the mountain tops. That is how I would have liked it to be but sadly, however hard I tried, the first hour of the day was a chilly, miserable business. I am not an early morning person at the best of times and clearly getting dressed, fed and packed in 20F is not the best of times.

Day 27, 3 miles short of Mormon Lake to 5 Miles before Marshall Lake, 22 miles

The enticing prospect of a monster breakfast at Mormon Lake Lodge got me on the trail in record time and I had covered the three miles by 8.15. Sadly the shop was open but not yet the restaurant so I had to make do with some pastries, mercifully not of the cheese and cherry variety I had sampled at Oracle, and two excellent cups of coffee – all American grocery stores seem to have coffee machines on the go as a matter of course. Meanwhile I was able to collect my post box which, much to my surprise, was waiting for me here in the middle of absolutely nowhere at probably America's smallest Post Office.

Mormon Lodge was a sizeable collection of dark brown wooden buildings on the shore of the non-existent Mormon Lake and housed a shop, the aforementioned tiny post office, a restaurant, a saloon and a sizeable museum dedicated to Zane Grey. Now to me Zane Grey was just a scribbler of commercial adventure novels and westerns, popular long ago in the way that Louis L'Amour had been in the 50s and 60s but now long forgotten in Britain. But in Arizona Zane Grey is regarded as some sort of folk hero, rather as

Mormon Lake Lodge

we regard Hemingway; literary giant, bon viveur, sportsman, hunter and fisherman. I came across his name all over the state and here, in addition to the museum there was a whole series of black and white photographs from the 1930s when he would use Mormon Lake as a jumping off point for his Arizona adventures.

Dotted around in the trees were quite a few accommodation blocks. It was a strange spot, a bit like an English seaside resort in March; everyone waiting for summer to arrive. The place had great charm though and you could imagine it filled with thousands of visitors for a rodeo or holiday weekend but on a grey, chilly morning the only visitors I saw were a young couple on a cycle tour from Flagstaff and an elderly couple having lunch, as is often the American way, at the odd time of 11.30.

Whilst I was chewing on my breakfast pastries the Lodge Manager, Scott Gold spotted me. He could not have given a bigger welcome to such a disreputable looking trail hiker cluttering up his place. In no time at all he had detailed a couple of his men to clean one of the showers for me, a facility that I was more than glad to avail myself of after three days of paddling through snow and mud. A further bonus was to be able to run my clothes through their Laundromat and so after an hour or so of hot water my clothes and I were both ready to face the outside world.

Part of that outside world turned out, somewhat unexpectedly, to be Larry Snead, one of the founding fathers of the Arizona Trail Association and Jan Hancock, a former Vice-President, who were at Mormon Lodge for a meeting of some sort. They were exceptionally welcoming and I think genuinely delighted to meet someone using their trail to its fullest extent.

We discussed Chris Townsend, who I told them had given me a great deal of good advice on the trail. Apart from his definitive book on walking the trail they mostly remembered him as the eccentric Brit who hiked much of the Arizona Trail in sandals, causing a great deal of head scratching amongst the local hiking community. But much of our talk was of the impending weather event – the storm I had heard about on the television weather forecast at Pine was gathering strength and Larry and Jan said that around a foot of snow was predicted for the next night, Saturday. They reckoned that if that happened it would make the trail impassable north of Flagstaff.

Clearly I might need to do some very creative thinking just to get to the Grand Canyon, let alone the Utah Border. With all that to ponder on I took a handful of maps into the restaurant as soon as it opened at eleven and tucked into a huge lunch. My priority now was to get into Flagstaff before all hell was let loose the next afternoon and with at least 35 miles still to go, any delay could see me spending a very unhappy Saturday night camping out in a snowstorm.

The day's walking was unremarkable. I left the sanctuary of Mormon Lake Lodge along the little road that ran beside the shore of the dried up lake. It was dotted with the occasional homestead but I fancied that few of them would be occupied at that time of year. Soon I was back in the deep woods that covered the flanks of Mormon Mountain, the low peak to my left. I was glad that

▲ *On the trail of the lonesome pine*

▼ *My constant companion, an Arizona trail marker*

for once the Arizona Trail had chosen not to go straight over a mountain. By now I had rather had my fill of climbing things.

Occasionally I caught sight of the San Francisco Peaks, the big range of mountains just north of Flagstaff that dominate the landscape for miles around. There was snow only on the very top of the range, which at nearly 13000ft is the highest point in Arizona so it was clear that Flagstaff had not had its usual quota of snow that winter.

After a couple of hours I left Mormon Lake behind on an excellent network of dry forest tracks that led northwards through pretty pine woods then across the Flagstaff road to Anderson Mesa, a flat open plateau of grassland and small trees dotted with mini versions of Mormon Lake, mostly with odd names – Potato Lake, Fisher and Fry Lake, Deep Lake and Horse Lake. Short of water when I reached the latter, I trudged across half a mile of mud before finding some not particularly inspiring murky brown water in a large puddle right in the middle. But mostly Anderson Mesa was stony ground and I walked on and on into the dusk before finding a patch that was free enough of rocks to camp on. At least it brought me within striking distance of Flagstaff, now probably less than fifteen miles away.

Day 28, Anderson Mesa to Flagstaff, 15 miles

I had been following the progress of the supposed approaching storm with a certain amount of suspicion. In the fortnight I spent at Apache Junction I had watched the neatly attired and immaculately groomed Arizona TV weather forecasters getting into a fair lather of excitement about some storm or other "likely to hit the Phoenix area" on Thursday. Thursday would come and go and all that would happen was that it would get a bit cloudy for a while, and then the sun would come out again. End of storm. It happened more than once. Not always on a Thursday, obviously.

But this one looked like the real deal. I woke to a bright red sky in the east which would have got the attention of any local shepherds had there been any (America appears to be almost sheep free, by the way). Dark clouds gathered all morning and a strong, chilly wind was getting up. It hurried me on across the flat plateau towards Flagstaff and the San Francisco Peaks beyond.

I passed the US Naval Observatory which was part of the Lowell Institute. It was there in 1930 that America discovered its first planet when a young Kansas astronomer called Clyde Tombaugh, who had come to the Lowell with no formal training whatsoever, somehow spotted Pluto, a faint point of light far out in the solar system. To some extent the discovery restored the observatory's reputation after its founder, the immensely wealthy Percival Lowell, made a bit of a fool of himself when he publicly declared that Mars was covered with canals built by the industrious Martians to carry water from its polar regions to the dry but productive central areas. Ironically, he also believed there was a ninth planet, but not exactly where Clyde Tombaugh found Pluto.

But all this was far from my thoughts just at that moment. The US

Walnut Canyon

Naval Observatory looked exactly like something you might see in England with a tea shop attached but not for the first time on the trail my hopes of some restorative refreshments were dashed. It was only there for the USGS to observe the clear unpolluted night skies, not for the public to look round.

Soon afterwards I reached a series of canyons including part of the impressive Walnut Canyon, a sort of mini Grand Canyon complete with sandstone cliffs in all hues of pink, grey and yellow. It was a lovely place and if I hadn't been in such a hurry to reach Flagstaff, I could have spent a fascinating afternoon exploring it further. I checked and rechecked the trail notes and maps, mindful of the fact that Chris Townsend, veteran of some of the world's most difficult trails, had inexplicably become comprehensively lost at just this point and had spent several frustrating hours casting around the canyons in an effort to find Flagstaff, a town ten miles wide from west to east. Now was not the time to make a route finding error.

Eventually the trail shot me out of the wilderness and under Highway 40 where giant trucks were ploughing their way east-west across the state. The Arizona Trail enters Flagstaff a little further east than I might have ideally liked and so I found myself walking through the modern industrial park area of the town for the best part of a couple of miles. On the way I spotted the Greyhound Bus Station and thought I might check out my options for getting out of town if the snow really came down and I became comprehensively marooned in Flagstaff.

Perhaps I have heard too many songs about the romance of taking a Greyhound Bus across America. At any rate I was certainly not prepared for the scene inside which looked more like a gathering of film extras that a US prison drama had rejected for being too rough. Everyone had huge quantities of luggage and they all seemed to be shouting at each other at once. Still, undeterred I wandered over to the desk to make an enquiry.

An unpleasant looking youth was engaged in an increasingly heated discussion with the desk clerk. Things were getting pretty lively when

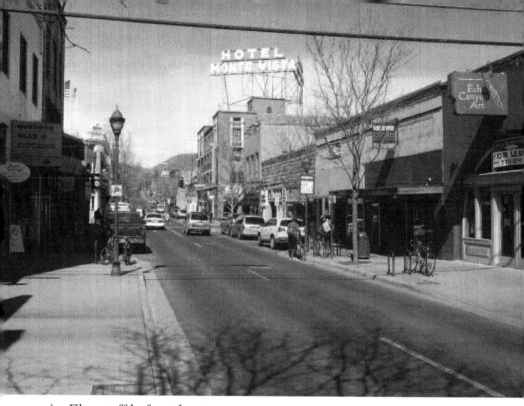

▲ *Flagstaff before the storm*

▼ *After the storm*

the desk clerk got up out of his chair, reached towards a drawer in front of him and uttered the slightly ominous words "Sir, I have to ask you to step back from the counter". I left before someone got shot and decided that I wouldn't be taking a Greyhound Bus anytime soon.

Finally I reached the town's lovely historic centre and called at the old brick built Monte Vista Hotel, which I thought might be more fun than a modern motel and just as cheap at $60 a night. Clearly lots of other people had come to the same conclusion as the hotel was completely full. However the receptionist was able to find out for me that the Flagstaff library was open and would be for at least another couple of hours, despite it being a Saturday afternoon. I needed to do some research.

Not for the first time I was struck by the quality and friendliness of American libraries. The lady behind the information counter turned out to be a trail steward for the Arizona Trail and was delighted to meet a thru-hiker. Despite that, American bureaucracy dictated that she needed to see my passport before I could use their internet facility and in reaching into the nether regions of my rucksack to find it, I bizarrely managed to injure myself for the one and only time on the entire trip. I somehow managed to cut the back of my hand on something hard in the pack and had to be bandaged up from the library's first aid kit so that I didn't bleed all over their books.

Nevertheless I still managed to spend a highly productive hour finding out just what lay between Flagstaff and the Grand Canyon, before checking in to the attractively named Highland Country Inn, which was neither an Inn, nor was it in the country. Rather it was one of several modern motels lining the legendary Route 66. It proved to be just what I needed and was run by a charming Indian called Henry with whom I had several good chats about cricket, something I hadn't expected to be discussing in Flagstaff or indeed anywhere in America come to that.

However much I love cricket, and believe me I happen to think it is the best sport in the world, the deficiencies of England's team in Sri Lanka seemed half a world away, as indeed they were. The approaching storm was what was occupying my thoughts and so I settled in to my room to get the latest news on the perpetually repeating Weather Channel. The news was not good – sometime in the night there would be 15 to 20 inches of snow dumped on Flagstaff, the snow would continue to fall through most of Sunday and there would be a slight improvement on Monday. After that things should perk up considerably.

Well, planning for all that could start tomorrow. For now I had a more important issue to take care of - namely a visit to the Beaver Street Brewery for a couple of pints of their exceptional beer and a large plate of food.

Days 29 and 30, Stalled in Flagstaff, No miles at all

I woke twice in the night and looked anxiously out of my motel window to see just what havoc was being wreaked by the storm. At 1.30 all was as before, not a flake of snow anywhere. But by four o'clock it was as if the motel had been picked up and dropped in the north of Canada. Thick snow lay over everything and was falling with an intensity that we seldom see in England. However, there was absolutely nothing I could do about it and so I went back to bed exceedingly grateful that I was tucked up inside and had not been caught out on the trail.

When I woke at dawn one look outside told me that I would not be going anywhere much that day, possibly for several days. It was an odd feeling to wake up and not be getting ready to head off north again. For weeks now every moment of every day had been about moving on – getting on the trail as early as I could, putting in as many miles as possible and only stopping when I absolutely had to. Even the resupply stops had been a flurry of activity – unpacking, sorting and cleaning kit and clothes, buying food and packing it for the next leg of the journey, sending e-mails, dealing with my post box and filling myself up with as much food as I could. Now I felt bereft of anything to do. Still, it was a major piece of luck that the storm had not come down when I was in the middle of nowhere and if I was to be kicking my heels around in filthy weather, Flagstaff was as good a place to be as any in Arizona.

Flagstaff is a town of 40,000 residents plus about 15,000 students, just big enough to have all the things you would hope to find in a city but not so big that you would ever feel swamped. Everywhere there are great little cafes, bars and music venues. The people look fit and there is a general air of bohemian cool such as you might find in one of the trendier parts of San Francisco. Altogether an excellent place for an ageing, would be hippie to get himself marooned for a couple of days.

Right in the centre of town are several streets of historic buildings and cutting through the middle of it all runs the railroad where freight trains a mile long clank their way through the little station seemingly for an eternity. Thankfully for the residents they had been stopped from blowing their horns a couple of years before but the huge wagons are still a great sight. You could imagine Jack Kerouac or Edward Abbey hopping out of a wagon, and indeed the latter did just that as a seventeen year old and spent the night in a Flagstaff jail for his pains.

No such problems for me though. I spent a couple of idle days wandering the snowy streets, and my goodness, you had to admire the endeavour of the town's residents who came out with everything they could muster from shovels to bulldozers in an attempt to keep the pavements and back streets clear. But they must be well used to snowstorms such as this one in a town built at 7,000ft with an annual snowfall of 80 inches.

Not being able to carry anything away with me limited my shopping possibilities but I did go out in the middle of Sunday's blizzard to poke around the mostly closed and deserted historic centre. Optimistically I bought a new pair of sunglasses, my third of the trip so far, and hopefully not containing the specially designed falling-out lenses that the first two pairs appeared to have been fitted with. I also found an old and, at $7 relatively expensive, copy of William Boyd's *Our Man in Africa*. As with all William Boyd's books it turned out to be a great read, quite different from any of his later stuff, a little like crossing Evelyn Waugh with Tom Sharpe. If you haven't tried any William Boyd, he is a well worth reading.

Macy's, a lovely old vegetarian café and bakery, proved to be a great spot to ride out the storm and I made several visits to drink their excellent coffee and eat big bowls of steaming soup and freshly baked bread, just the place to hang out if you have plenty of time on your hands. It was full of interesting looking types sitting around reading papers and books, doing stuff on their laptops or just chatting. Nobody seemed to be in much of a hurry to rush home and do all those dull domestic chores that so occupy most of our lives.

The evenings were spent at the bar of the Beaver Street Brewery, a sizeable place which brews several different types of strong and flavoursome beer in their own microbrewery and serves excellent food to hundreds of people each day. One evening I chatted to the manager who told me how he despaired of America's reputation for making rotten beer, largely the fault of the big corporations such as Budweiser, Miller, Coors and Michelob. The Beaver Street Brewing Company and microbreweries all over the States were doing their level best to fight back, he told me. As always I found everyone in there very friendly, ready to strike up conversations at the bar and amazingly interested in what I was doing. I wasn't sure if a lone hiker from America would get the same kind of reception walking across England.

Snow fell in plentiful abundance all day Sunday but by Monday the storm was all but played out and by the afternoon the sun had come out again. Apart from the best part of three feet of snow covering everything, Arizona was back to its usual sunny best.

Meanwhile I had been poring over my maps and doing more research at the library. I reckoned I had a cunning plan to keep the walk going towards the Grand Canyon. I could see that if the centre of Flagstaff was like that, the Arizona Trail would be completely impossible to find for at least a week, let alone be passable, but I believed I had found a solution. Running more or less parallel to the Arizona Trail and leading up to the Grand Canyon was Route 180, a busy but not hopelessly busy single lane road. The map showed almost nothing on the roadside all the way to Tusayan, just short of the Grand Canyon. In fact I remembered driving down it two years before and my memory suggested lots of pine trees and empty space and that it was not one of those American roads with a fast food outlet every forty yards. That would mean precious little in the way of water sources, probably none at all on one section for more than thirty miles.

My internet session in Flagstaff Library had miraculously revealed three places to stay along Route 180 if it proved impossible to camp. They were fairly well spread out along the route at 21, 52 and 78 miles from Flagstaff. The only seriously challenging day would be the 31 mile stretch to reach the road junction settlement at Valle at mile 52 but with nearly three days rest in my legs I felt that it should be doable, although such a distance straight up a main road in one day might not feature highly in my list of "Great Walks I Have Done".

I called at the first place on the road, concerned that they might not be open at this time of year, the intriguingly named Shooting Star Inn, where the normal B&B price was $225, just about the amount I had been paying for five nights up to now. But their unique selling point was that the owner, Tom Taylor was a big expert on astronomy and gave his guests a free visual tour of the stars as part of their package. Tom was delighted to hear from a fellow hiker and offered me a special rate, $150 including dinner, still higher than I was used to but his place looked very nice and, if it kept my trip going, it would be more than worth the cost.

Although Highway 180 was still closed on Monday, my second full day in Flagstaff, it was scheduled to reopen on Tuesday morning. The forecast was good for the rest of the week and, all being well I would reach the Grand Canyon by Friday lunchtime. I had no idea if the Canyon would be open. If not, that would be that – a bus to Page or Las Vegas and an early plane home.

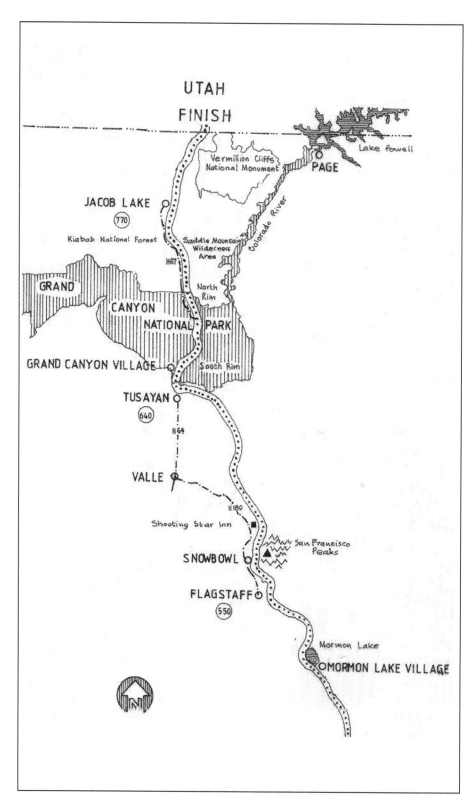

Chapter 11

ROAD RUNNER

FLAGSTAFF TO THE GRAND CANYON, 81 miles

*"All endeavour calls for the ability to tramp the last mile, shape
the last plan, endure the last hour's toil. The fight to the finish
spirit is the one characteristic we must possess if we are to face the
future as finishers"*
Henry David Thoreau

Day 31, Flagstaff to Shooting Star Inn, 21 miles

The 51 mile walk up Highway 180 reminded me of one of my old
school reports which read "Jeremy sets himself low standards which
he consistently fails to achieve". I thought that a road walk of this
length would be a bit dull and, boy oh boy, was this ever dull? If
I tell you that to keep myself amused I resorted to timing myself
between the mile markers all the way up to see if I could complete
each mile in less than twenty minutes, that will tell you just how
little there was to keep my mind occupied.

I was sad to leave Flagstaff. There are not many places that make you
think to yourself, "I could live here and be very happy" but Flagstaff
is one of those; just a lovely, relaxed, Bohemian town that has all you
could want from the place you live (except perhaps better weather).
Before leaving Route 66 to head north I treated myself to another fine
breakfast at a Hispanic-run diner just along from the Highland Country
Inn, took a couple of pictures of the giant icicles hanging off their roof
and headed off through Flagstaff's pleasant looking suburbs.

San Fransisco Peaks

Snow was piled high everywhere, 36 inches of it according to that morning's newspaper. The storm had dumped down nearly half the winter average in a day and a half. But it was a sparkling morning, dazzlingly clear and bright and the views through the snow laden pines to the San Francisco Peaks were spectacular. Just three days earlier approaching Flagstaff from the south I had only seen a dusting of snow on the very top of the peaks but now they were covered in the stuff. The weekend's blizzard was the first snow since before Christmas and so half the town had taken Monday off to drive up to the Arizona Snowbowl, just twelve miles out of town, for what might prove to be their last chance to ski that winter. The road was packed with vehicles.

Late morning I stopped at a little chalet motel just opposite the entrance to the Snowbowl to see if I could buy a coffee and cake and fill up my water bottles. The manager said no, I couldn't buy anything but that I could take whatever I wanted from the remains of their breakfast buffet for free, which was even better. Whilst I

141

enjoyed a couple of cups of coffee and some pastries I was joined by an elderly Phoenix man who had given up on the idea of skiing for the day. He said that there were simply too many people up there and that he would try his luck the next day when the crowds had died down.

Beyond the Snowbowl the traffic mercifully thinned out. I passed nothing of any interest all afternoon apart from the Flagstaff Nordic Centre, which must have gratefully sprung into action that week after a lean winter and further on I saw a young couple trying to snow shoe in the woods. Since snowshoeing had been one of my options for getting north, I was interested to see that they were struggling to make much forward progress in the light, powdery snow.

In Flagstaff I had sought some advice at Babbitt's, the best known of the town's many outdoor stores. I asked them about snowshoes and they didn't think that I wouldn't be able to do such a long distance with a pair, particularly if I wasn't accustomed to using them. They thought I might be able to cover ten or twelve miles a day at best.

Shooting Star Inn

Plodding on up the road I reached the big open expanse of Kendrick Park at around four o'clock. The Shooting Star Inn was supposed to be there but it was far from obvious which of around a dozen properties spread out over several square miles the Shooting Star Inn might be. After a couple of false starts I knocked on the door of the only property I could see smoke coming from and was directed to a substantial pine building about half a mile up the track.

Not surprisingly for a Monday night in the middle of nowhere, surrounded by three feet of snow, I was the only guest but still got a great welcome from Tom Taylor and his newish partner Amy, who had moved to Arizona from Maine about six months before. Tom had built his house right there solely because Kendrick Park's almost uniquely dark night sky made it a great place for stargazing and he had run it as a successful Bed and Breakfast for eight years. The huge open plan living area was full of giant telescopes and all the decoration was moon and star themed.

The house was entirely self-sufficient in power, getting all they needed from a 48 volt solar photovoltaic unit. That sounded wonderful and I wistfully thought of my own £7,000 a year fuel bill in North Norfolk. Less good was the fact that water had to be fetched from Flagstaff each week and the next morning Tom was due to drive in and collect another 500 gallons in a tank on the back of his pick-up. But I fancied that if you lived in such an isolated place, you might be grateful for any old excuse to pop into town.

Tom was something of a Renaissance Man. As well as running the astronomy related B&B, the Shooting Star also had a photographic studio where he worked on his prize winning photography and upstairs on a mezzanine floor I could see a recording studio where he played music with his band, The Cosmic Rocket Band. Before I left, Tom gave me a copy of their latest album and I noticed that he had co-written all the songs and played lead guitar as well.

Amy cooked us a superb dinner of pork chops, asparagus and mashed potato – real food and the first plateful of European style food I had seen for more than a month. We all sat together and talked hiking, B&B, Edward Abbey, the Grand Canyon and all sorts of things that

143

we found we had in common. I am sure that we could have talked all night but I didn't want to outstay my welcome so I left them in peace and headed to my room to finish off Stieg Larsson.

After an excellent breakfast, and I felt a little guilty at getting my delightful hosts up at 7.15, I headed up the road for the 31 mile trudge to Valle. And my goodness, what a trudge it was. The road was almost arrow straight all the way – a couple of times I walked a seven mile stretch without a single bend of any sort. For readers in Norfolk imagine walking up and down the Holt by-pass for eleven hours and you will know what sort of a day I had. For readers elsewhere, use your imagination!

I became more than a little irritated at times by motorists getting too close for comfort. I was walking on a sort of meter wide hard shoulder on the left hand side of the road facing the oncoming traffic. Most drivers pulled out to give me some space but others were not so thoughtful. Sad to say, and it was far from a scientific survey, it seemed to me that women drivers were much less likely to give me room than men. Not having much to think about, I pondered on why that would be. Maybe it was that whole Men Are From Mars spatial awareness thing, maybe they just didn't much like the look of me.

The countryside became flatter and more open as the road dropped down to 6000ft and the snow was less deep but there was little of interest to look at. The only event that shook me out of mind-numbing monotony was when a passing motorist stopped in the middle of the road and asked if I was hiking the Arizona Trail. That struck me as an odd thing to ask someone who was in the middle of Highway 180 but I politely explained what I was doing.

Then the driver surprised me by saying "Jeremy, right?" It was Li Brannfors, Trail Steward for the Grand Canyon section. Months before we had swapped several e-mails. Li had turned out to be something of a map geek and had sent me online an extraordinarily valuable treasure trove of detailed Arizona Trail maps.

He was on his way to Flagstaff to pick up a friend who he would then take to Phoenix Airport, a round trip of some seven hours. I would find out a few days later that this sort of kindness was typical of the man and also that he was clearly not averse to long road trips. By fortunate chance, Li lived at the Grand Canyon Village and so he gave me his phone number and we promised to hook up when I reached the Canyon on Thursday night or Friday morning.

I reached Valle tired and footsore from the hard tarmac around half past six. It was an unassuming place, to say the least, a spread out collection of motley buildings at the junction of Highways 180 and 64. By now the snow was much thinner than it had been at 8000ft but the ground was still either snow covered or muddy and so I gratefully checked in to the only place in town that appeared to be open, the slightly swish looking Grand Canyon Inn. I felt that after the day I had just put in, I deserved a bit of comfort. "Because you're worth it", as those irritatingly self-satisfied cosmetic adverts suggest.

Day 33, Valle to Tusayan, 23 miles

With the prospect of my third and final road trudge ahead of me, I didn't exactly leave the comfort of the Grand Canyon Inn with much anticipation for the day ahead. Highway 180 had become Highway 64 which for its speed and the sheer unwillingness of its drivers to give me more than half an inch of space made the 180 look like an English country lane.

About a mile outside Valle a slim, deeply tanned man dressed in immaculate running gear came trotting up behind me and slowed to a walk. I took him for a weekend jogger out from the motel for a nice easy mile up the road then back for a big breakfast. "Where are you heading for?" he asked with a distinctly Australian twang to his accent.

With some pride, I gave him a run down on my trip and asked, more out of politeness than real interest, "What about you? Where are you off to?" "Oh, I'm running round the world" he calmly replied in a tone of voice that suggested that such a thing was perfectly normal behaviour. From somewhere in a neat little waist pack he produced a card headed "Tom's Next Step" with Guinness Book of Records/ Oxfam Charity/Donate Now printed further down.

To say that I was absolutely flabbergasted would be putting it mildly and for the next 60 minutes we ambled up Highway 64 whilst I fired a million questions at him. I can't think of another hour on the trail that passed so quickly.

Tom Denniss was a wave power pioneer and businessman from Sydney. He had set out from there 4000km earlier with his wife Carmel and friend Libby who were gamely acting as his back-up team and the three would be on the road for at least 18 months whilst Tom took a scenic route through Australia, New Zealand, America, Canada, South America, Europe and Asia. He was running at least 25 miles a day and appeared totally untroubled by the 4000km he had already covered. He looked as fresh as a daisy.

After an enthralling hour I let him go and watched for ages as the slight figure disappeared into the distance up the interminably straight road. Since then we have swapped a few e-mails and he is currently in Spain, still going well and now comfortably over half way through his epic. If he finishes, he will be only about the seventh person to run round the world. I had met another of the Magnificent Seven some years ago, the delightfully eccentric Rosie Swale Pope. She and I were competing in the six day stage race called the Marathon des Sables. She was clearly completely bonkers even then and subsequently went on to run round the world in five years, doing it the hard way with no back-up and crossing some very difficult regions indeed. Tom Denniss, in contrast, appeared to be completely sane.

An hour or so later a car pulled up just ahead of me and two women got out. "Jeremy" they called. It was Carmel and Libby who had been tipped off by Tom to look out for me. They lavished me with food from their cool box and we made promises to try and hook up at the Grand Canyon, which sadly never quite happened.

I had just chomped Carmel and Libby's sandwiches and fruit when

▲ *Tom Denniss, only 15,000 miles to go*

▼ *Off Highway 64*

another car pulled up and a man ran across the road proffering a foil-wrapped package. "We brought you a BLT" he called. The day was turning into Meals on Wheels.

I didn't recognise him at first but it was Shooting Star Tom minus the straw cowboy hat that he had mystifyingly worn throughout my visit, including during dinner and breakfast. He and Amy were on their way to the Grand Canyon with a couple of friends in search of lunch and to put down a marker for some Backcountry Camping Permits, without which you were not allowed to camp in the Grand Canyon. Soon I would need to plead with the allegedly difficult Park Rangers to let me have one.

After that I walked the remaining fourteen miles without being offered any more food, which was just as well since my stomach had now taken on the shape of a beach ball after all this largesse. Tusayan, a sort of gateway town to the Grand Canyon National Park loomed large at around four o'clock and after all the emptiness of the road, came as something of a shock.

I passed a small airport from which a myriad of travel companies ran flights over the Canyon. Helicopters and light planes filled the skies with noise and soon I arrived at a busy looking strip of hotels and restaurants. The next day I would discover that there is a refreshing lack of tackiness at the Grand Canyon itself and perhaps to some extent Tusayan serves as a buffer to keep some of the usual hotel and restaurant chains at bay. I found one of the few non-chain cafes in the town and stopped for a cup of tea and a cookie.

Tea, by the way, is something that Americans do not do very well at all. Mostly you are offered a Styrofoam mug filled with not quite boiling water and a rather feeble tea bag on the side. You won't be offered milk but if you ask for some they will try to put the milk into the mug of hot water before you have had a chance to do anything with your tea bag. The net result is generally weak and lukewarm at best. If you want a decent cup of tea in America, you need to take control of the making of it yourself. I could see why most Americans only ever drink coffee.

I decided to pass over the seductions of Tusayan and its hotels and restaurants as an evening stop over. The snow there was only lying around in pockets and so on the north end of the town I was able to pick up the Arizona Trail for the first time in 75 miles. It felt good to be back with my old friend and sparring partner again and I enjoyed walking a mile or two further on before making camp for the night in a delightful forest clearing.

After five days of comfortable beds, good food and ample beer I had become a bit too soft. If trail conditions would allow me to find a way through to Utah, I very much wanted to complete the trip in the proper style.

Chapter 12

GRAND CANYON INTERLUDE, 16 miles

"The region is, of course, altogether valueless. It can be approached only from the south, and after entering it, there is nothing to do but leave. Ours has been the first and last party of whites to visit this profitless locality. It seems intended by nature that the Colorado River, along the greater potion of its lonely and majestic way, shall be unvisited and undisturbed"
Lieutenant Joseph C. Ives, 1858

Day 34, Tusayan to the Mather Campground, 6 miles

The Grand Canyon is almost unique amongst the world's great natural sights in that until you have practically fallen into it, you have absolutely no idea that it is there. From the south you approach the Grand Canyon National Park through miles and miles of forest. On the few occasions that you get a view into the distance the Canyon itself just does not show until you are right there, which makes it all the more astonishing when you actually get to see just what all the fuss is about. I would defy anyone catching sight of the Grand Canyon for the very first time not to stand there with their mouth hanging open slackly for at least half a minute. It is a genuinely jaw-dropping moment.

A pleasant six mile stroll through the woods from my campsite in the Tusayan woods brought me straight to the Mather Campground without getting lost, which I felt was a pleasant surprise. The Grand Canyon Village is notoriously difficult to find your way around – all the roads curve round on themselves, which means that you can unwittingly arrive back exactly where you started from fifteen minutes earlier and, until you reach the South Rim itself, it is so heavily wooded and featureless that you can't really see where you are.

I had booked ahead for the Mather Campground whilst marooned in Flagstaff. The Grand Canyon National Park doesn't allow wild camping, which is probably fair enough but when I saw that most of the 400 sites at the campground were empty, I realised that I needn't have bothered booking ahead at this time of year. Still, my pitch only cost a few dollars and it was well worth it for the nearby shower and laundry block.

I had seen the Grand Canyon a couple of years before, albeit somewhat briefly and so I decided not to rush off for another look but to spend the afternoon on the more immediate business of getting hold of a Backcountry Permit. Without one you are not allowed to camp a night inside the Canyon and, however early you start, you can't realistically expect to get down to the bottom and then up to the North Rim in a day. Besides, hiking through the Grand Canyon is something be savoured, not rushed. But the Backcountry Permit is notoriously difficult to lay you hands on. Most are taken up months in advance and for the Arizona Trail thru-hiker, that presents a logistical problem – for somewhere you will reach at least five weeks into the trail, you can only have a vague idea that far in advance just when you will get there. You can only book for one of the two campgrounds for a specific night. I expected to have some problems with all this which might have left me hanging around for a few days. With flights home scheduled for just over a week's time, I couldn't afford any delay.

I found nearby Market Plaza, a square with a small hotel and a couple of decent looking shops and restaurants, without any difficulty and retrieved my post box for the last time on the trail. From there I took one of the extremely convenient (and free) shuttle buses that ply their way around the Grand Canyon Village all day in a partially successful attempt to discourage motorists from doing the same.

The bus dropped me right outside the Backcountry Information Office. I thought about entering on my knees, ready to beg and plead for any leftovers, scraps and cancellations at any campground for any day in the next week. But ideally I wanted to spend the next day, Saturday, having a rest, sorting out my kit and having a touristy look along the Rim Walk. I also thought that if I could delay going through the Canyon for another day it might give the snow more chance to melt. So I tentatively asked the Ranger for a place at Cottonwood Camp, about fourteen miles along the trail and part the way up to the North Rim, for Sunday night.

After a very long pause and much pressing of buttons on his computer keyboard the answer was "Yes, we could do that". Hallelujah! To my delight and amazement, within an hour of arriving at the Grand Canyon Village, I was all sorted out and ready to go on through to the Utah border, 110 miles away. Perhaps the snow had put a lot of people off or maybe it was still quite early in the season. Whatever the reason I felt very lucky to have struck gold.

The only fly in the ointment might be snow or weather conditions. There were sizeable pockets of snow still lying around at the South Rim which was 7000ft high and the North Rim was more than 8000ft, rising to 9000ft on the higher parts of the Kaibab Plateau beyond. I asked the Rangers what the conditions were like up there but they were pretty hazy about current snow levels. It seemed that nobody really went up the North Rim at this time of year and that it wouldn't be officially open until late May. They could tell me though that there might be some rain on Sunday night, which would mean more snow at the higher levels.

That evening I arranged to meet Li Brannfors at the splendid El Tovar Hotel, the smartest place to stay in the Grand Canyon Village and by some distance the oldest. Perched precariously on the South Rim, the El Tovar opened in 1905, an interesting blend of Swiss Chalet and Scandinavian Hunting Lodge, and is little changed to this day. The plush interior made me feel very scruffy indeed but Li and I took a table in the bar which was a great deal more casual than the smart dining room. The bar looked out on a lawn which in turn looked out on the Grand Canyon. What a place to stay.

Li lives at the Grand Canyon Village and has worked for several years on a job which is something to do with stopping and containing forest fires and dealing with the aftermath if they get out of hand. I never fully grasped exactly what his role was but rather liked the sound of it nevertheless. It must be wonderful to spend so much of your time looking after the wilderness but I did wonder about the isolation. Although the village was constantly thronged with day visitors, not many people live there and the nearest town of note is Flagstaff, more than eighty miles away.

We shared several plates of the El Tovar's lavish portions of nachos and salsa together with a few excellent beers. Mostly we talked about the Arizona Trail which Li had plenty of strong views on and he was very interested to hear my thoughts. He could not have been more helpful and I think he saw it as his duty as a Trail Steward to give as much assistance as possible to thru-hikers. He was delighted to hear that I had managed to get a Backcountry Permit, particularly as he was working hard on the Backcountry Office to make the whole system more convenient for Arizona Trail hikers. We made a plan to hook up again the next evening.

Day 35, Grand Canyon Tourist, 10 miles

"Golly what a gully",
William Howard Taft, U.S. President 1909-13.

With my precious Backcountry Permit tucked safely in my pocket and a bit of time in hand to get to the Utah border if the North Rim was passable, I could afford to spend the day enjoying the South Rim as a tourist and so, after breakfast at the Market Plaza I took the shuttle bus several miles along the South Rim for a gentle, pack-free sightseeing stroll back to the Grand Canyon Village.

The view across to the North Rim some fifteen miles away and the floor of the Canyon more than 4000ft below was truly staggering but after a couple of jaw-dropping miles where every twist and turn of the trail revealed another monumental vista, it was easy to feel almost satiated by natural wonder. Besides, I think that I felt that sauntering along

▲ *Tourist for a day*

▼ *What a gully*

the Rim would pale into insignificance compared to the day I would have tomorrow walking down to the bottom.

I pottered about the village for a while and, despite all that I had read, I found it refreshingly free of tackiness. The little train from Flagstaff pulled right into the middle of it, as it had done for nearly a century, there was a large and quite smelly area bang in the middle where dozens of horses used for the tourist treks into the Canyon were kept and a few tourist buses pulled in and out. But apart from the El Tovar and couple of other lodges, together with a very small cluster of souvenir shops, I thought it mercifully free from anything overtly commercial.

How easy it would have been to have built a line of huge hotels along the Rim, all with Canyon view rooms, but walking along the South Rim the village and its lodges were almost invisible until you were right on top of them. Equally somebody sometime must have thought it a brilliant idea to run a couple of cable cars down into the depths but again, good sense had won the day*. For once I had to congratulate the powers that be for showing admirable restraint and hardly spoiling the place at all.

Most of the rest of the day was spent in an idle kind of pottering about way, eating, washing kit and returning my post box to the Post Office on Market Plaza, but I did have one important piece of admin to look after. The Arizona Trail finishes bewilderingly in the middle of nowhere and if you haven't arranged for a lift out to one of the towns about forty miles away, Kanab or Page, you are in for a long wait for a passing motorist, or a long walk.

Before leaving England I had called one of the two numbers on the Arizona Trail website for people who supposedly provided a shuttle service away from the end of the trail and rather thought that I had pretty much arranged everything with a lady called Betty Price. I had given her my approximate date for reaching the end of the trail

---

* Apparently the Navajo Nation currently has a plan to run a cable car into the Canyon from somewhere along the East Rim, which would bring them a staggering $70 million a year. Needless to say, the plan is meeting with much opposition.

and said that I would call her from the Grand Canyon and then Jacob Lake, thirty miles from the border, to give her the exact time that I would arrive there.

So I headed for the bank of payphones at the Mather Campground armed with a couple of phone cards for what I felt should have been the simple task of confirming my schedule. Needless to say, as is often the way with payphones, all did not go quite according to plan. First of all my phone cards did not want to work for Betty's number, then after numerous attempts to get through, they both ran out. When I called the card provider they said that they could only be renewed from my home phone. I politely explained that I was camping at the Grand Canyon, that my home was about 8000 miles away and possibly also pointed out that if had been calling from my home number I wouldn't be needing to use one of their bloody phone cards from a payphone, would I? When the Customer Services Operative, or whatever he was called, patiently repeated "I'm sorry sir, you can only renew your card from your home phone" I tested the durability of my forehead with the receiver for the second, and not the last time that day.

Half an hour later after a visit to Market Plaza I was back at the phones with a brand new card. After getting cut off three times in a row, I finally spoke to an elderly lady who identified herself as Betty's mother. She confidently said that she could handle Betty's business. I told her exactly what I was doing and about the calls I had made from England to her daughter. She then perplexingly said that they would need to know where I was leaving my car. I explained again that since I had been hiking the Arizona Trail on foot from Mexico I didn't have a car at which point she told me to call back in five minutes, which I did. Five minutes later I found myself going through exactly the same conversation again almost word for word just as if the first call had never happened.

This clearly wasn't going anywhere so I managed to establish that Betty would be back home later that evening and said I would call back then. Later I didn't get much further with Betty herself who turned out not to be available on the day I expected to get to the Utah border but said that she might be the next evening. I said I would call again from Jacob Lake but it looked as though I might have to rely on the goodwill of any motorist who might happen to stray into the remote Utah border region.

Meanwhile a couple of people had arrived on my shared patch of the campsite having obviously hiked in from somewhere. I guessed they must have been down the Canyon so I went over to ask them where they had come from. "Mexico", they said, to my utter astonishment.

It turned out that Alex Mackie from Fife and Kristin Gates from Alaska had started out separately and between two and three days after I had left the Mexican Border. They had joined forces after a couple of weeks and had hiked together the rest of the way. All the way along the trail they had been a couple of days behind and had been picking up rumours of an Englishman called Jeremy who was up ahead. With my three day stop in Flagsaff and my extra night at the Grand Canyon they had finally caught up. I decided that thru-hikers are like buses – you wait five weeks for one to come along and then two arrive at once. Apart from Mike Elliot at Patagonia who was hiking the trail in two or three sections and the couple by the Gila River, I hadn't met anyone all along the Arizona Trail apart from a handful of day-hikers near the cities.

They had been caught out in the snowstorm near Mormon Lake and both looked pretty well exhausted from the trek. Getting to Flagstaff in the worst of the storm must have been horrendous but I was a little mystified as to exactly how they had managed to find the trail north from Flagstaff. However they were both carrying snowshoes, which must have helped to some extent.

It seemed an extraordinary coincidence that the only people thru-hiking the Arizona Trail that spring had all started out not knowing about each other just three days apart and would all end up on the same small bit of the Grand Canyon campground at the same time. Later the coincidence reached the realms of absurdity.

Alex, Kristin and I went out with Li for a pizza in Tusayan and on the way back I discovered that all three of us had all been at St

Andrews University. Alex had left a couple of years before having done a degree in Philosophy, Kristin had come over three years ago for a term from the States and back in the dark ages I had read Ancient and Medieval History during four blissfully happy years on Scotland's east coast. There are coincidences and then there are things that simply defy belief. That the only three people thru-hiking the Arizona Trail in the spring of 2012 should all be from the same small Scottish University and should set out within three days of each other was such a remote chance as to be utterly absurd.

Alex and Kristin had also managed to acquire permits for Cottonwood Camp so we made a plan to join forces for the next day at least.

Chapter 13

THE END IS NIGH

ONWARDS FROM THE GRAND CANYON, UTAH BORDER 110 MILES AWAY

"I love to be alone. I never found a companion that was so companionable as solitude"
Henry David Thoreau

Day 36, Mather Campground to Cottonwood Camp, 17 miles

"There's nothing quite like the Grand Canyon. No matter how many gorges and valleys you have seen, the Grand Canyon will seem novel to you." John Muir

I have to confess that until I started doing some research for my journey, I didn't really know what the Grand Canyon was all about. Two years before I had taken a brief look at it, stood with my mouth open for a bit, uttered a few inanities along the lines of "Wow, it's huge", walked along a little further, then took a few pictures and got back in the car. That is pretty much all that most people who visit the Canyon ever do and so it felt like a real privilege to be able to walk right through it from one side to the other.

I had learned some basic facts about the Grand Canyon; that it is 280 miles long and between four and fifteen miles wide, that it was formed by millions and millions of years of erosion by the Colorado River and that if you know what you are looking for, and frankly I don't, you can see a layer-by-layer record of the planet's geological history going back 20 million centuries. The exposed rocks at the bottom by the Colorado River date back two billion years, which, rather like the National Debt of Greece, is a tricky figure to get your head around.

Today I would be going down into it, right to the bottom 4500ft below the South Rim and then up the other side, 5500ft up from the Colorado River to the North Rim. It is without doubt right up there in most walkers' top ten of "The World's Best Hikes" so Day 36 was going to be the highlight of the entire trip and it was great that the Arizona Trail saved the best until last. I had been looking forward to this day all the way from Mexico.

We would be going down the South Kaibab Trail, a switchback path that from a distance appears to be descending a cliff. I was more than a little worried about just how steep it might be and whether it would be covered in snow and ice. As it turned out, I needn't have worried. All the way down it was a beautifully kept, wide and smooth trail, never steep, and with no stomach churning drop-offs and apart from a few patches near the top, no snow at all. I don't think I had an easier morning's walk all along the Arizona Trail.

Li, bless him, had clearly made an early start to the day. On our way to the South Kaibab Trailhead we found a packet of maps that he had prepared for Alex and Kristin attached to a post in the middle of the trail just before the trailhead. However, it would have been impossible to go the wrong way down the South Kaibab Trail. For one thing, if you are not on the trail you have probably fallen over the side but otherwise there were plenty of people heading up and down it, including several large groups on horseback coming back up from the bottom who we nervously stepped aside for. They were doing the climb the easy way for their legs, the hard way for their bottoms – those western saddles did not look at all comfortable to me. Half way down we reached a plateau where most of those hiking into the Canyon thought better of going any further on the premise that they already had to climb back up 2500ft and didn't much want to add another 2000ft to that, however lovely it all was. The traffic thinned out dramatically from there on down.

Mule train on the South Kaibab Trail

And my goodness it was lovely, every single step of the way to the bottom. Breathtakingly beautiful swirling rock formations, plunging canyons and giant cliffs all dressed up in the most extravagant colours under the sun. We stopped over and over again to take photographs, each new corner revealing a view that demanded recording. I think that of all the photographs I took on the trail, about a fifth were taken on that morning.

The nearer we got to the Colorado River the more beautiful it became, a crescendo of greens from the grey-green of the ancient rocks through the vibrant green of the new spring vegetation to the murky blue green of the fast flowing river. Oddly, the Colorado River, which I have just described to you as blue green, was named by the Spanish for its red colour. But the red sediments that gave it its natural colour are now trapped behind the dam at Lake Powell. The whole business of the taming of the river by man-made dams has been a hugely controversial issue since the 1950s. Wilderness enthusiasts and early environmentalists were bitterly opposed to the damming of the Colorado by the Glen Canyon Dam and remain so to this day. To read about what the river was like before it was dammed, there is a great chapter in Edward Abbey's Desert Solitaire about his journey through the Canyon in a cheap rubber boat shortly before everything changed.

Right at the bottom the Kaibab Trail crosses over the Colorado and begins the long climb up to the North Rim. We paused a while at the Bright Angel Campground and chatted to a group of river rafters who had pulled their boat up on to a nearby sandbank. Rafting trips are hugely popular and quite expensive. They involve floating down the Canyon in a rubber raft, sometimes for a couple of weeks and pulling in now and then for a hike or to camp for the night. My feeling about lively, fast-flowing water is that it is probably best viewed from a bank and that once you've seen one set of rapids, you've seen 'em all. Although I could see a certain appeal in their trip, I preferred mine.

At the bottom of the Grand Canyon

A little further on we passed through Phantom Ranch where you can stay the night and also treat yourself to a meal that by American standards is quite staggeringly expensive. But I suppose that if you are going to carry your shopping 4500 vertical feet and ten miles by trail, you may want to charge a bit for the end product and when your nearest competitor is half a day way, you can probably get away with it.

The long climb up the North Kaibab Trail started in earnest at Phantom Ranch as the path entered a sharp sided canyon known as The Box, chiselled out by the fast flowing snow melt of Bright Angel Creek. It was all very splendid but on a dull, grey afternoon something of an anticlimax after the wonders of the morning.

By now Alex, Kristin and I had established a pattern that would become the norm over the next few days, namely not walking together much. I think that I had become too used to my own company and my own pace to easily fall in with anyone else's for very long and I noticed that whereas my routine was to stop every hour to take off my pack, drink some water and perhaps eat a trail bar, they liked to keep going, then stop for a long break at lunchtime. I would find them lying by the side of the trail, boots and socks off and most of the contents of their packs strewn around – both had brought a staggering amount of food away from the Grand Canyon and I rather envied them their copious quantities of bread, salamis and cheeses whilst all I carried with me were my meagre rations of porridge, trail bars and noodles.

In contrast to the plentiful nature of his provisions, Alex appeared to have no extra clothes with him at all, no warm gear to put on in camp whatsoever, whilst I was parading around each evening looking like the Michelin Man. He must have been frozen. Or perhaps being Scottish helped and Kristin coming from Alaska would have found the chilly Arizona nights positively balmy. Kristin, I had discovered, had left her New York banking family to work in Alaska for a while as a dog musher, which I think means shouting a lot at a team of huskies so that they pull a sled in the direction you want them to. Alex was working on a Scottish estate where he looked after the deer and probably the stalking thereof. They were both, despite their combined age adding up to less than my 53 years, hardened trail veterans who had already ticked off several of the big trails including the 2600 mile Pacific Crest Trail.

By the time we all met up late in the afternoon at the Cottonwood Campground we had already climbed 1500ft in 7 miles. Tomorrow we would need to ascend another 4500ft in the same distance before going up over the North Rim on to the Kaibab Plateau, the last challenge of the journey. Wild camping would have been perfectly possible in all sorts of places on the North Kaibab Trail but I could see why the authorities might want to discourage it. For now Cottonwood camp with its small washroom building, empty Ranger's Hut and a few spread out camping pitches would do us fine.

It had been a really memorable day's hike and I would urge anyone to go to the Grand Canyon whilst their legs still work. Book in to the El Tovar for a couple of nights and walk down the South Kaibab or Bright Angel Trail to the bottom. Don't go on any further; turn around there and walk back up to the South Rim in time for beer and nachos at the El Tovar bar. It will be one of the most mind blowing days you will ever have.

Day 37, Cottonwood Camp to De Motte Park, 26 miles

I woke early at Cottonwood Campground to leaden skies and low cloud hanging sullenly over the North Rim. The night had been the warmest of the entire trip with the temperature dropping no lower than a positively balmy 54F but the morning did not look all that inviting. Despite that, Alex and Kristin were packed and away at the unfeasibly early time of 6.30, possibly to accommodate a long lunch! By then the clouds were tumbling down the cliff faces around the camp and rain began to fall, the first I had seen since setting out from Mexico.

Arizona was looking more like the Scottish Highlands and I imagined that Alex would be feeling right at home on such a morning. But I

Heading up to the North Rim

found it hard to get going and fiddled about with my kit in driving rain until I had got myself thoroughly wet. Mercifully it turned out to be no more than a brief shower and passed over just as I was setting out on the 4000ft climb to the North Rim.

My trail notes gave no clue as to what lay ahead and the description of what proved to be just about the scariest path I have ever set foot on merely said "Pass a small, developed rest area with water and restrooms and then continue another 2.5 miles to reach the North Kaibab Trailhead.

Let me tell you what it was really like for someone like me with a poor head for heights. Soon after leaving Cottonwood the trail left the lively and fast flowing Bright Angel Creek to turn northwest up a steep sided canyon, which all looked pretty much like the sort of thing I was expecting to see. What I was not remotely prepared for was the way that the trail then abruptly started climbing the cliffs to my left in a surprising and improbable way. In no time at all it was squeaky bum time for Jeremy.

The North Kaibab Trail was a phenomenal piece of trail building by the National Parks Service in the 1920s but I honestly have no idea how it could have been built. The trail was about six foot wide but it felt more like six inches and it was just simply cut into the side of a sheer cliff. Again and again I would look ahead to see where the trail might be heading as it disappeared round the next bend. Often it would seem impossible that it could go any further but then it would turn the corner and continue its precipitous upward march.

On one side was the canyon wall, on the other sphincter clenching drops of 500ft or more. I shuffled along like a condemned man, determined not to stumble and become another Grand Canyon statistic. Roaring Springs Falls came and went almost unnoticed; I was too busy watching my feet which for an hour or so appeared to be suspended inches away from disaster.

Finally the torture ended as the trail reached a little bridge, switched from one side of the canyon to the other and climbed up some clay cliffs which were substantially less sheer. From the bridge to the top was probably another 2000ft up but I could not have been more relieved to make such a climb in my life. The last couple of miles had been a huge test for me and I felt that I had passed with, if not exactly flying colours, then a small gold star.

The trail passed through the Supai Tunnel. I had been warned by a Ranger at Phantom Ranch about a rock fall at this point but it proved not to be significant enough to impede my progress and afterwards the muddy track switchbacked through pinon-pine and juniper woods all the way to the top. More ominously it was also cutting through increasingly heavy snow and I started to fret about what I might find on the Kaibab Plateau at the top. Would the trail be passable or would I, horror of horrors, have to return down the terrifying path I had just climbed up? That thought, I think, was of more concern to me than the realisation that I might not be able to finish the trail.

With much relief I finally crested the North Rim around 11 o'clock.

▲ *The North Rim*

▼ *So that'll be the trail then*

A couple of minutes later I found Alex and Kristin sitting by the side of a large, empty car park, totally clear of both cars and snow. But all around was deep, deep snow, as thick as any I had seen since the Snowbowl north of Flagstaff. My companions were happily tucking into their bread, cheese and salami so I went off in search of the continuation of the Arizona Trail. In no time at all I found the trail sign but it was buried up to its neck, if signs can be said to have a neck, and there was at least three feet of snow lying across the trail.

This, I reasoned, was probably why the North Rim is officially closed until at least the middle of May to all except those foolish enough to attempt to come through on foot. Everything except for the road and the car park were buried deep underneath the white stuff and we would find out later that the only reason the tarmac is kept free of snow is for the Rangers and Grand Canyon National Park staff who live at the North Rim. Li Brannfors, we knew, kept apartments at both the North and South Rims, about fifteen miles apart as the crow flies but a staggering 225 miles by road.

The choice was simple. However dull it might be, and boy was that walk ever dull, the road would have to be our lifeline to the north for at least the next forty miles until the Kaibab Plateau dropped down a little from 8000ft around Jacob Lake. Alex and Kristin were clearly settled in for a long lunch so, plans made, we agreed to meet up somewhere along the road later and I trudged off gloomily, trying not to look at the road sign that read "Jacob Lake 41".

Water was going to be a serious problem as all our potential water sources were near the deeply buried trail. Besides, streams and ponds were not going to be visible under all this snow and if they were, they would most likely be frozen solid. I had filled up my bottles in the Bright Angel Creek just before starting up my old friend the vertical cliff trail but most of that had gone by now. However I expected to pick up some at the Grand Canyon National Park entrance in about ten miles time, if not before.

I arrived there about mid-afternoon after nearly four hours of pleasant, if slightly monotonous ambling through the silent, snow buried forest.

There was no sign of life (or water) at the park entrance and a weather forecast chalked on a board was for November 27th, which was not a particularly promising sign given that it was now late March. There were a few small houses nearby but I didn't bother exploring them – there were no tracks of any kind leading to them from the road so I guessed that they too would be unoccupied until May.

Clearly I couldn't wait that long for a drink so I stuffed some snow into my bottles to see how long it would take for it to melt (the answer, it turned out, was a very, very long time) and headed off up the road, Highway 67.

Beyond the National Park boundary the road became almost arrow straight as it cut through a flat, wide bottomed valley of (probably) grassy meadows know as De Motte Park. To show how flat it was, there was even a landing strip marked on my map, just beside the road. A couple of miles along, my water problems were solved for the time being when I spotted a trickle of murky brown snow melt in the gutter by the side of the road. I managed to fill a couple of bottles and left a note in the middle of the empty tarmac telling the others about it in case they missed it.

A few miles further up any hopes of food, water and possibly even a bed were dashed when I reached Kaibab Lodge and its nearby country store and gas station. They were all firmly boarded up for winter. The trick now was to find a place to put a tent down that would be reasonably snow free and flat and just as dusk began to fall and I was getting more than a little desperate, I spotted a flattish shelf of grass, free of snow and just big enough to pitch three tents on. Alex and Kristin rolled up about twenty minutes later.

Sixteen miles of road walking was not quite what we had in mind when we reached the North Rim but we had made considerable progress towards the Utah Border. The Jacob Lake Inn was only 24 road miles away and all being well, we should be able to reach it the next day.

Cold camping at De Motte Park

Day 38, De Motte Park to Jacob Lake, 24 miles

The night time temperature in our snowy home dropped to 19F, not perhaps as cold as we had feared but, given that our pitch gave us no shelter whatsoever from the sneaky wind blowing across De Motte Park, it was cold enough to persuade Kristin that she needed to be on the move at 6 o'clock to get some warmth through her bones.

Alex and I took substantially longer to get moving. Not for the first time on the trail I found myself staggering about stiffly in the freezing morning air struggling to get moving. As usual, I found packing up on such a cold morning a thoroughly miserable business, frozen fingers battling with clips and zips and tight stuff sacs. There would be much about the journey that I would miss but cold mornings I would not miss at all. I should have done better with my choice of gloves and a supply of those little tea bag hand warmers would have gone down really well.

When we finally got underway the road was deserted, dead straight and tree lined, not perhaps a day's walking to gladden the heart but it would take us to within thirty miles of the end of the trail if we could reach Jacob Lake that day, 24 miles away. I walked with Alex for an hour or so and it was good to have a little company after so many solitary weeks. But we soon caught up with Kristin who, despite her early start, was not far ahead. In no time at all my routine of stopping every hour meant that the others moved inexorably away from me and I found myself in one of the most eerily silent places I have ever been in.

I was walking through a huge area of fire damage, the biggest I had seen all along the Trail. Forest fires are a real hazard in Arizona and can be caused by the slightest thing in the bone dry summer heat – mostly careless campers or motorists, but many by lightning strikes. Rangers are employed just to sit all summer long at the top of watchtowers and look out over the surrounding forests for any sign of smoke in the surrounding forests.

For six miles I walked through a landscape of charred tree trunks. The wind had died to nothing, no birds or animals had found a home in the burnt forest and the road was totally empty. I felt like the father in Cormac McCarthy's The Road trying to find any sign of life in the post-apocalyptic landscape. Mostly I was amazed that six years after the fire, the forest showed so few signs of life but apparently it can take much longer than that before things return to any kind of normality.

Late afternoon I came upon the others spread out lavishly by the side of the road and we walked on to Jacob Lake together where to our great delight the Jacob Lake Inn was open for business. It reminded me a little of Mormon Lake, a collection of timber buildings stuck in the middle of absolutely nowhere for no apparent purpose. With the opening of the North Rim still a couple of months away, things were obviously far from being in full swing but the large family who appeared to be running the place were there in force.

We were thrilled to get out of the snow and pamper ourselves with showers, warm beds and real food and, to my great delight, Lumberyard Red Ale from Flagstaff. I am afraid that in my trail weary state by the time I had drunk three cans of it, getting back to my room without making a nonsense of myself proved somewhat tricky.

We sat at the bar over our burgers and beer and planned an exit strategy. Betty Price was not looking to be the answer to our prayers - barring unforeseen disasters, we would reach the Utah Border in a day and a half with ease. Using Betty's shuttle service would leave us stranded there without any water for at least a day. Li Brannfors had kindly suggested that he needed to make a trip to his apartment on the North Rim and could then pick us up at the trailhead that marks the end of the Arizona Trail. A couple of phone calls on Kristin's mobile (so much easier than my phone cards, I have to admit) secured a meeting with Li for Thursday lunchtime. We were all set and for the very first time I felt confident that I would finish the trail.

My sun terrace at the Jacob Lake Inn

Day 39, Jacob Lake to Winter Road, 19 miles

The next morning we made an oddly sluggish exit from the Jacob Lake Inn. Alex and Kristin were clearly in no hurry to leave and didn't emerge from their rooms until I had already demolished my last plate of bacon, eggs and pancakes on the trail. After breakfast they both disappeared back to their rooms only to reappear at about 10.30 to potter about the Inn's souvenir shop and buy ice creams.

Meanwhile I sat outside fretting somewhat, probably without good reason since we only had to notch up about 19 miles that day, but I was so used to getting on the trail early that hanging around outside the Jacob Lake Inn for an hour just did not feel right. By the time we finally left shortly after 11 o'clock I had come to the conclusion that although it had been great to have some company and swap stories about the trail, I preferred to set my own pace. They too had probably grown used to each other's company and routine over the weeks and I was very aware of that slightly unsatisfactory dynamic that often occurs in a group of three where two of group are closer to each other than the third. That and the fact that they probably thought I was a bit of an old fart.

A couple of miles northeast of Jacob Lake along Highway 89 we were able to pick up the Arizona Trail again. It felt like meeting up with an old friend and it was great to leave the tarmac behind. Out of the last 150 miles I had walked about 120 on the road and I really had not come to Arizona to walk up roads, but they had served their purpose when the trail was impossible to follow.

Snow still lay about in profusion but if we were careful we could follow the line of the trail through the pine forests and small canyons. Despite the snow and quite a lot of mud it was very pleasant walking and gave us a reminder of what we had been missing for the last forty miles. As soon as I stopped for a water break I fell behind and lost Alex and Kristin totally until around lunchtime when I rounded a corner and found them surrounded, as usual, by the entire contents of their packs, boots and socks off

173

and clearly settled in for another long lunch break.

We chatted for a while but I was keen to carry on and so we agreed to camp near the track called Winter Road, nine miles or so down the trail, the other side of a clearing in the forest that seemed to go on for ever. The trail had been descending gradually all day and we were now down to about 7000ft, leaving the snow behind for the very last time. For four or five miles I crossed a strange, open area of low sagebrush, juniper and creeping prickly pear, flat as a pancake and oddly monotonous.

It gave me plenty of time to ruminate, as I had been doing for most of the day, on the imminent end of the trail. It was strange to think that in 24 hours I would be whisked away from the trailhead and deposited in Page to wait nearly four days for my plane to Las Vegas.

Odder still was the fact that in less than a week I would be back home in Norfolk, probably straight into my usual workaholic routine of multitasking for England. With my Bed and Breakfast getting into full swing for the Easter holidays there would be shopping, cooking, cleaning and gardening to do, two months' worth of personal e-mails to take care of and Parish Council and North Norfolk Beach Runners meetings to attend on my first two evenings home. England would be playing cricket in Sri Lanka and the US Masters Golf would be just about to start.

All part of a rich, busy and wonderful life but I knew that I would miss the simplicity of life on the Arizona Trail. St Francis de Sales knew what he was talking about when he said *"When I am busy with the little things, I am not required to do greater things"*. For six weeks all I had to do each day was to make sure that I break camp in the morning, pitch camp in a suitable spot in the evening, walk as many miles as possible in between and fill myself with enough food and water to sustain the effort. Okay, so there had been a few issues with boots and snow but for forty days life had been wonderfully uncomplicated. That was what I would miss so much.

SOLITUDE

"I thought it'd be great. I figured out I'd have, like, time alone with my thoughts. But you know it turns out I don't have as many thoughts as you'd think".
Joey in Friends

Something I thought about a lot before starting the Arizona Trail was just how I would get on being totally on my own for so long. If you have managed to read this far, you may be under the misapprehension that the hike was just one long social. That could not be further from the truth – mostly I went days without seeing anyone to talk to, three days on one occasion without even seeing any sign of human life, however distant.

Before I set out I thought that I might be driven mad by the solitude and silence. Those who know me will tell you that I find it difficult to be quiet for long and if there's nobody about to talk to I work with a radio or television on for company, sometimes both at the same time in different rooms. I wondered what it would be like to be divorced from the 24-hour media that so envelops my day to day life. I am not quite like my parents, who when I was growing up liked to watch the six o'clock news and then the nine o'clock on the basis that something different might have happened that needed their attention, but I do like to know what is going on in the world.

If I sit down at home to a lunchtime sandwich I will be reading a newspaper and probably watching television as well. When I did some walking in the weeks before coming out to Arizona, I always carried a little portable radio to keep me company. Sometimes I would switch it off for a while to see what it was going to be like on the trail without noise in my ears and I got bored very quickly. As I move around the house I leave a trail of radios switched on as I go from room to room. In short, I find it difficult to get by without a cacophony of sound in my life.

I thought about bringing a little radio with me but wondered if I would be able to get anything on it except country music stations with endless adverts for businesses in places I was never going to get to. Or perhaps an iPod with some good music on it or some audio books, but to my eternal embarrassment, I have no idea how to use such a thing or how to download anything onto it. It was all I could do to learn how to use my camera, camcorder and SPOT; one more gadget and my brain might have gone into meltdown.

As it turned out, I needn't have worried. Aside from the road days, I honestly do not think I was bored for an instant. There was always something to look at and always plenty to think about. All day my mind would be nicely occupied with thoughts, not exactly earth shattering ones but important to me nevertheless; route finding considerations, where to get the next water and whether my bottles would last out until then, how far I could walk by midday and where I would get to that evening, where I might camp and would there be water there? The evenings in camp were short and pleasantly filled with eating, smoking, reading, writing and looking at maps.

If it all sounds pretty trivial, well I suppose it is but I don't think being bored and lonely ever entered my head, nor, I am sorry to say, did any thoughts on a higher plane.

Alex and Kristin caught up with me after I had found a decent little clearing in the scrubby woods just beyond a track called Winter Road. I had a good look around the area but there appeared to be no water at all within reach. A couple of stock ponds were dry and according to the trail notes, there were no water sources from here to Utah. This was probably the driest region I had walked through since the Sonoran Desert – we would just have to make do with what little we were carrying until Li picked us up tomorrow.

The others made a big fire and sat by it well into the evening, playing cards and being generally rather jollier than I felt like being. Somehow

Last camp

the fast approaching end to the trail was making me feel unusually introspective and I decided somewhat uncharitably that I might have preferred to be camping on my own for my very last night in the wilderness.

Day 40, Windsor Road to the Utah Border, 11 miles

I wish I could tell you about the glorious, grandstand finish to the walk but it would be hard to imagine a greater anticlimax than finishing the Arizona Trail. The moment of triumph I had been imagining through nearly two years of planning and forty days of hard slog across Arizona turned out to be the damp squib of all time.

Perhaps I had looked forward to the finish for too long or perhaps I have grown accustomed to enthusiastic crowds cheering every competitor across the line at most of the running races I have ever been in. My last tough long distance race was the Mont Blanc Ultra, 105 miles of the most seriously mountainous trail you would ever see. The finish was in the old market place at Chamonix and with about a mile or so to go I passed a German girl who was clearly in some trouble. We only had about 20 minutes to get in before the race's cut-off time so I told her to stick with me and I would see her in to the finish.

Fifteen minutes later we came into the main square, packed with cheering crowds, brass bands, cow bells. You name it, it was all there. We crossed the line together. Mrs B was there, as was Jimmy Markwell who I had run much of the race with. The German girl said to Mrs B "Thank you for lending me your husband", Jimmy handed me a warm beer and a roll-up and I think we all probably burst into tears with the emotion of it all.

Now clearly I couldn't expect any of that sort of stuff in the middle of absolutely nowhere but the end of the Arizona Trail, as you will see, lacks a certain something. Perhaps the last few days along the road from the North Rim followed by thirty miles of gentle, downhill forest paths was too much of a wind down in itself. For a truly gritty finish the trail should end at the top of a particularly rugged mountain or after crossing a dry and rocky desert. But I guess they are not going to move the border, so thru-hikers will just have to learn to love what is there.

The final day began early for two of us at least. Kristin was away at 6 o'clock again whilst I was still poking my dozy head out of my sleeping bag. But I managed to get on the trail not long after 7, at which point there was absolutely no sign of life from the still slumbering Scot. Alex eventually woke up at 9.30, by which time Kristin and I were very nearly home and dry.

The going was gentle and pleasant, winding through small, shallow juniper filled canyons before finally breaking out of the trees just as the trail dropped down below 6000ft for the first time in many weeks. Tantalising views of the great rock formations and cliffs of Utah began to appear and I saw for the first time the stunning rose-coloured Vermillion Cliffs to the Northeast.

I caught up with Kristin resting under a bush and together we walked the last couple of miles of easy, downhill trail. Perhaps I was too busy looking for the finish line or admiring the Vermillion Cliffs but it was there, within half a mile of the finish that I fell over for the one and only time in 800 miles. The flapping laces on one boot attached themselves to the cleats on the other and the net result was that the boots came to a standstill whilst I carried on. No damage was done except to my dignity.

Soon after my comedy pratfall a rather grand trailhead complete with attractive ramada-style picnic pavilions, barbecues, table and benches came into view. For some bizarre chivalrous reason I urged Kristin forward so that she could be the first thru-hiker to finish the completed Arizona Trail but I asked her to come back and film me going through the border in glorious triumph.

Five minutes later Kristin came back saying that she couldn't find the end of the trail. For ten minutes or so we wandered aimlessly around the empty campground expecting to see a huge sign announcing something like "End of the Arizona Trail. Congratulations to thru-hikers". But nothing appeared. We sat down under one of the pavilions to ponder the situation. Eventually a family appeared in a huge RV and so I walked over to ask them if they knew where the Utah Border was. They weren't sure but thought it might be somewhere down the road leading out of the trailhead.

We walked a few hundred yards along the dirt track and indeed there it was, a knee-high wooden board with "Entering Utah – Leaving Arizona" inscribed on one side. "Well, that must be it then", we said. And with that the journey was over.

An hour or so later Alex appeared and we sauntered back down the road to our little sign and took a few pictures just to show that we had made it to the end. But I think that we were all suffering from the same feeling of anticlimax and a little bit of "What now?"

Around 2 o'clock Li Brannfors turned up fresh from a marathon

▲ *The big finish*

▼ *With Kristin Gates and Alex Mackie at the finish*

drive all the way round the outside of the Grand Canyon just to do a couple of chores at his North Rim apartment and to help us out. He really is one of the kindest, most thoughtful people you could ever meet – there was an ice box in the back of his pick up containing North Rim snow to chill coke, lemonade and some beer celebrating Arizona's recent centenary. He had also brought freshly-baked cookies and some excellent tortilla chips and dip for us. I hoped that people appreciated his kind nature. It worried me a little that he did so much to help people that it would be easy for him to be taken for granted.

An hour later we pulled up outside the US Post Office in Page where I would collect my post box for the very last time. Alex and Kristin were getting a lift from Li all the way to Flagstaff but for me it was the end of the road. We all said our goodbyes doing that oddly British thing where you try to embrace each other in a manly sort of way and end up making a mess of it, treading on toes or pulling away too early. As a nation we don't do embraces all that well.

Standing in the middle of a huge car park in a strange town, wondering what the **** I was going to do there for nearly four days and watching my trail companions drive away in the direction of the delights of Flagstaff just added to my all-pervading sense of gloom. I had known exactly the same flat feeling after finishing very long races and this had been a long race in spades. Tomorrow I might feel brighter but for now I would just have to give in to the gloom.

> *"I made it through the wilderness,*
> *Somehow I made it through"*
> Madonna, Like a Virgin.

AFTERWORD FROM PAGE

"As you get older, the questions come down to about two or three.
How long? And what do I do with the time I've got left?"
David Bowie

After Li and his charges had disappeared up the road towards Flagstaff I wandered about the wide streets of the little town of Page looking for a suitable motel to spend the next four nights, thinking that four nights was at least three more than I wanted to spend there. Page was chock full of motels of all sorts ranging from some quite grand looking places to ones that looked frankly dangerous. There was even an entire street called The Street of Little Motels in what was billed as Page's Old Quarter. Given that the oldest bit of the town was built in 1960, I surmised that maybe Americans can do irony after all.

Eventually I settled on the very pleasant looking Rodeway Inn, mostly because I could see that some of their rooms had large and commodious balconies directly facing the afternoon sun. After the last couple of decidedly chilly weeks, time spent loafing about in the sun would be just the thing. Amazingly they only wanted to charge me a paltry $40 a night which included some sort of breakfast and free use of a computer. I happily parted with an amount of money for four days that I would charge for one night at my Norfolk Bed and Breakfast.

I still felt oddly grumpy though and so after sprucing myself up a bit and putting on my clean town clothes I took myself off to a very nice looking Mexican restaurant to cheer myself up. The plan backfired when I stumbled on possibly the only two waiters in America who looked better suited to a comedy double act. Laurel and Hardy would have been proud of these two.

Buffoon A took my order for a much needed beer and a full ten minutes later Buffooon B brought me a glass of Coke. Both then completely ignored me for at least twenty minutes so I could neither clear up the beer/coke confusion nor order any food. In typical British suffer-in-silence fashion I stoically sat there glaring at my unwanted Coke and occasionally flapping my arm about in that half-hearted fashion that we all do to attract waiters who never seem to be looking in our direction.

When, much later, my food eventually arrived, Buffoon B rushed off leaving me with absolutely no cutlery to eat it with. Nearly ten minutes passed, by which time an otherwise excellent meal had gone stone cold, I finally managed to attract the elusive eye of Buffoon A and get some utensils. My later request for a cheque (bill) was comprehensively forgotten so I went up to the cashier, got slightly huffy and paid up leaving just a 10% tip, which in America is tantamount to a gross insult.

A small point poorly made but it somehow corresponded with my oddly black mood on what should have been a day of great celebration.

The next day I felt a bit like Forrest Gump when he started running across America and found he couldn't stop. After nearly six weeks of perpetual motion I was programmed to get up, pack up my stuff, start walking and only stop when it got dark.

But first thing I was a little bit more Forrest Grump when Mrs B woke me with a phone call at 6 o'clock, forgetting that Britain had just put its clocks forward an hour for British Summer Time. Mornings are not my best time for cheery chit chat and on this particular morning I was neither fully awake nor fully over the previous day's anticlimactic gloom.

Needless to say, for want of anything better to do and because I couldn't help myself, I went walking again. I had discovered that Page had an eight mile trail that circumnavigated the town and so I just had to walk it before I did anything else. And very fine it was too giving great views of the surrounding cliffs and mesas and of course Lake Powell itself. I loved the feeling of walking without a big pack on my back for the first time in six weeks.

Next I went to the nearby Dollar Store and bought a small pair of scissors and a pack of razors. Back in civilization I was finding my wild appearance of long blonde hair and bushy pepper and salt beard less amusing than it had been out on the trail. It took me a good hour, first of all with the scissors and then with several razors, to restore order to my face and I rather wished I had just gone to an old fashioned barber and handed the whole thing over to him. My face looked a great deal thinner than I remembered it, as indeed it was.

I took my freshly scrubbed countenance off to explore the town and found it to be an endearing but very odd place in several ways. First of all, despite sitting on a rocky plateau in the middle of an equally rocky desert, Page is a massive boating centre. As the first town going east on the 186 mile long Lake Powell, boatyards, boat builders, repair and storage facilities and boat rental depots are everywhere.

Fifty years before, neither Page nor Lake Powell were there until in the 1950s plans were made to dam the Colorado River at nearby Glen Canyon in order to tame the Colorado's natural flow and provide water for the burgeoning cities of Phoenix and Tucson. Page sprang up solely to accommodate the huge army of construction workers needed for the project and the azure waters of Lake Powell were the result of the Glen Canyon Dam being built. The damming of the Colorado was hugely controversial at the time and remains so to this day.

I went to have a close look at it and found it impressive but as an environmentalist I could sympathise with wilderness supporters who strongly object to the taming of a once lovely river. They have a valid point but I also suspect that vastly more people derive benefit from having water coming out of their taps than would ever have enjoyed the Colorado as it once was. After all, I had just crossed much of Arizona's wilderness and hadn't seen a great deal of evidence of people out there making use of it. If you don't use it, you lose it, I thought.

The other oddity of Page is the line-up of twelve impressive and prosperous looking churches on Lake Powell Boulevard, all in a row. When Page was being built the Bureau of Reclamation gave land to every denomination that wanted to build a church. So one after another come the Catholics, Methodists, Southern Baptists, First Baptists, Lutherans, Latter Day Saints, Episcopalians, Nazarenes and so forth, each structure large and beautifully kept, twelve churches for a town of around 5000 people. I wondered why you need so many different churches when, let's face it, they are all talking to the same God. Or am I missing something?

Right opposite the row of churches is Page's sizeable high school and I couldn't help thinking that there can be nothing more calculated to produce a town full of atheists than going to school each day right opposite twelve churches. It can be no coincidence that the school's football team style themselves The Sand Devils.

My days in Page passed by extraordinarily quickly and much more pleasantly than I had feared at first. The grim mood that I had brought into town evaporated rapidly as I walked the Rimview Trail each day, sat in the spring sunshine, read several books and ate a great deal more food than my thin body had become used to.

On the final morning I treated myself to my very last American breakfast and walked down to the town's little airport. I was quite sad to see the back of the place. The lengthier than expected stay in Page had given me the chance to recharge my batteries and get ready for whatever the next few weeks might throw at me.

Apart, that is from the flight away from Page. For sixty minutes of sheer, abject terror the plane ride to Las Vegas took some beating. Anyone who knows me will tell you that flying frightens me more than anything going. I have no idea how the damned things stay up there and little confidence that they will do so for very long. People keep telling me that flying is much safer than driving a car. That may well be so but every time a plane hits the tiniest bit of turbulence I imagine it falling out of the sky in a whining, spiralling dive whilst 400 passengers all scream at the top of their voices.

Believe me, you really do not want to be sitting next to me on a bumpy plane. Whilst everyone else is calmly sipping Bloody Marys and reading the dreary in-flight magazine, I am the one gripping the seat in front, sweating profusely, muttering "Let me of this ****ing thing" and wondering why nobody else realises that we are all just about to spend the last two minutes of our lives being entertained by a shrill, wing-splintering plunge to earth.

That is exactly how I felt all the way to Las Vegas on Great Lakes' little 19 seater. I knew things weren't going to be quite to my liking when the pilot came through and spoke to us just before take-off and said something like "We are expecting more turbulence than usual today. We have brought on board an extra box of sick bags and there will be an opportunity to purchase clean underwear before disembarking at Las Vegas." Actually he only said the first bit but the rest might have been helpful too.

All the way to Vegas, and bear in mind that it was a perfectly clear day, the bloody thing bounced around like some sort of badly adjusted fairground ride. I sat at the back and held on to anything I could whilst the rest of the passengers seemed utterly unconcerned about the terrible fate that was clearly about to befall us. Never have I been so glad to land in all my life and, believe me, I am always glad to land.

After the horrors of that hour, seven more in transit at Las Vegas and then the overnight flight back to London were a breeze. So when anyone asks me "What was the worst thing about doing the Arizona Trail?" I have to tell them that it was the flight from Page to Las Vegas. Next time I shall walk it. It's only 300 miles.

IMPRESSIONS OF AMERICA AND AMERICANS

"There are many wonderful things about the United States of America that deserve praise – the Bill of Rights, the Freedom of Information Act and free book matches are three that leap to mind – but none is more outstanding than the friendliness of its people."
Bill Bryson, Notes from a Big Country

The great Alastair Cooke was still working on his thoughts about America after more than fifty years of brilliant broadcasting so perhaps it is somewhat presumptuous of me to come up with a few glib generalisations after walking across just one state. After all I was only there for two months and for much of that I didn't meet anyone for days on end. Let's face it, an American might not learn much about Britain by walking the Cornish Coastal Path, for instance.

However, I just wanted to stick up for our much-maligned cousins. I can't help thinking that we in Britain are probably a bit too quick to criticise a country and a people that many of us know less about than we think. We have all seen American tourists in Europe and it's easy to poke fun at them with their noisiness, their guide books, their endless quest to read every notice going, their foolish questions and their general lack of understanding of European ways. Like a five day old kipper, they don't travel all that well.

But I'm not sure that we Brits have all that much to be proud of when we go abroad. We can be spotted a mile off with our socks and sandals, our white "holiday trousers" brought out every year whether or not they still fit, our inability to learn even a few words of anyone else's language, our perplexing need to continue eating

British food all over the Mediterranean and our unparalleled ability to spend an entire fortnight away sunburnt and drunk.

It may seem palpably obvious but most Americans are only truly comfortable in their own environment. Yet we still poke fun at them for being brash, ignorant of the world, over-religious, obsessively consumerist, warmongering and intolerant and unable to elect even half-decent leaders. We also hold the belief that nobody in the USA has a sense of humour, which is odd given how much American comedy appears on our screens.

Well, all I can say is that of the people I have met on my journey from fleeting encounters in shops, motels and restaurants to lengthier talks with people such as Ann Caston or Mike Elliot in Patagonia, or those who have been kind enough to acknowledge my waving thumb, or Pop C in the Rincons or Li Brannfors at the Grand Canyon, all have been delightful, helpful and fascinating people, genuinely interested in what I was doing. I do wonder if a lone and scruffy looking American would be met with the same kindness, thoughtfulness and openness from we reserved Brits.

As for Arizona and perhaps by extrapolation America itself I become more and more taken with the country at each visit. The USA and its people have a wonderfully positive self belief which nigh on fifty years of relative stagnation has hardly put a dent in. Americans seem to be born with an unshakeable belief that they can and one day will succeed with their lives, no matter what happens along the way. Negativity is a concept that just doesn't seem to exist. They love their country too – everywhere I went I would see the Arizona flag and the Stars and Stripes flying proudly, outside public buildings and private houses alike. In Britain we seem to have become an unduly pessimistic and cynical country and as for patriotism, the sight of a house flying a Union Jack or Cross of St George is mostly likely to lead you to the door of a dangerous right-wing bigot than a genuine patriot.

Perhaps also America is a country where being poor is not as disastrous as it might be in Britain. Living at or just above the minimum wage may be easier in so many ways. The minimum wage in Arizona is $7 an hour, in California $10. Not much of a wage on the face of it, but for an hour's work you can put more than two gallons of petrol in your car, in Britain you wouldn't even manage one on our minimum wage. Housing is so cheap that if you were to save all of your minimum wage for two years you could buy outright a perfectly serviceable park model (prefab house) which would do you well for most of your life. Try doing that in Britain for £20,000.

Food, alcohol and cigarettes are all noticeably cheaper and electrical goods substantially cheaper than in Britain and schooling at state level is generally more reliably consistent than ours. The sharp elbowed middle classes don't feel the need to jockey for position to find somewhere decent to send their children. Nearly every school gives a decent education. Public services seem to be well-run and greatly respected (a rookie cop in Phoenix earns $50,000 a year, enough to buy a very decent house in the suburbs from just one year's salary).

I suppose, though, that not all is well even in a burgeoning state like Arizona. A great number of people, particularly in the Hispanic communities, seem to get by at a sort of subsistence level. They have little or no safety net of welfare benefits along the lines of the British model and for many Americans the question of health care is the big elephant in the room. You really, really do not want to get something seriously wrong with you if you don't have proper insurance cover. The ongoing problems of the Native American population are a whole story on their own.

But maybe the lack of welfare and a National Health Service encourages more people to work and to work harder and with a better attitude than we have in Britain. It is easy to sneer at the "Have a nice day" culture but I can honestly say that in eight weeks in Arizona, I came across just the Dorito girl at Roosevelt Lake and the Laurel and Hardy waiters in Page who were not giving their jobs 100% effort. We could learn a great deal from America on the virtues of friendly and helpful service.

Could I live there? Well quite probably but I would need to find somewhere not as hot as Phoenix in summer or as cold as the Colorado

Plateau in winter. But with their absurdly tempting property prices, I could probably afford to have a place in each and plenty left over besides. I'd probably be back in Britain in no time, though – all that upbeat enthusiasm would get me down in the end and I'd need to come home every now and then for a dose of good old British cynicism. And let's face it, baseball just isn't cricket.

EQUIPMENT AND OTHER MATTERS

Stats and health

Although I wasn't using any GPS measurement, I can't have walked from the Mexican Border to Utah without clocking up 800 miles. Possibly a few more with diversions here and there and the amount of extra miles I walked in the not particularly compact resupply towns. The walk took forty days, although there were four days (one in Pine, two in Flagstaff and one at the Grand Canyon) when I stayed put, which means that I averaged over 22 miles each walking day. Once I found my trail legs I was doing comfortably more than twenty miles each day. The smallest distance for a walking day was 6 miles into Pine and the longest was 31 miles up the dreaded Highway 180 into Valle.

I can't tell you how many feet I climbed because I never totally got to grips with that feature of my Timex WS4 watch. Although it did tell me what my altitude was at any given moment, I just couldn't quite fathom out how to get the information about accumulated height gained and lost. However from the records of other thru-hikers the total climb on the Arizona Trail is supposed to be somewhere around 92,000ft, and I have no reason to suppose that I did much less, although the road walking may have ironed out a few bumps towards the end. That means an average of nearly 2,500ft climbed each day, most of which came in the first half before Pine and the Mogollon Rim.

I expected to have all sorts of health issues and before I set out I was fascinated to see just how my body would react to ten hours of hard exercise every day for nearly six weeks. I needn't have worried though. Apart from some problems with blisters, which were fairly easily resolved by some strategically placed Compeed, and some bottom issues on three separate occasions caused by drinking half a gallon of milk in quick time, my body just got stronger and stronger every day. There was a bit of a hiccough when I was struggling with my Walmart boots and my knees, heels and back all started to protest but otherwise for a beat-up old runner's body, it lasted me pretty well.

Carrying a pack proved to be much less bother than I had expected. When you first put on a fully loaded pack you think you will never be able to move two yards without toppling over, let alone all the way to Utah. But in a few days you feel quite at home with the weight and, apart from those days when I had to carry a load of extra water, I hardly noticed it was there. It was always very nice to take it off, though, and I would do that every hour to stretch out my shoulders and upper back.

I finished the trail feeling fitter than I had been for many years and really enjoyed dropping so much weight. By the end I had built up a lot of muscle and dropped about a stone and a half. Sadly that did not stay off for long. After six weeks of starving myself my body finally said enough is enough and for weeks after getting back to England I ate everything in sight and I was soon back up to my usual 13 stone.

Equipment

I am a little hesitant about writing reams of stuff about my kit. After all, I can't ever remember asking anyone what they took in their suitcase when they went on holiday so why would anybody have any interest in the contents of my pack?

But you never know, if my book inspires just one person to take to the trail, any trail, that would be good enough for me. And that person may well want some tips on the best stuff to take with them. I am not going to totally satisfy the kit geeks out there because I have no intention of lacing the next few pages with technical spec about weights, materials and so on. All that sort of thing is out there on the net anyway.

When I hatched my plan to walk the Arizona Trail, I possessed no camping kit at all aside from a couple of Therm-a-rest mats which had been used for three days on the Cornish Coastal Path many years ago but they were too bulky to take to Arizona, so I had to start from scratch, which was not only a steep learning curve but quite expensive as well. Outdoor kit can be bought very cheaply, I found, but the best stuff, which pretty much means the lightest stuff, comes at a fair old price. Over the year or so of collecting gear together, an equal amount of the contents of the house went on e-bay to pay for it all!

I did a great deal of research and in no time at all became a total kit geek. The internet was a great tool but some of the internet review sites were of dubious value. Having just settled on the best sleeping bag, say, because someone had written "Brilliant, I slept out on the top of Everest in the Super Warm Soft Downie Z3 for six weeks and it was amazingly warm", the next review would say "Worst bag I have ever had. Froze to death in a Super Warm Soft Downie Z3 in the South Downs in August". Confusion reigned over every item but in the end I decided that if it was made by a good company and was light enough, then it would probably be man enough for the job.

I took a lot of tips from TGO magazine, The Great Outdoors. Their gear section is edited by Chris Townsend, who had hiked the Arizona Trail in the spring of 2002, albeit a month or so later in the spring than I was setting out. Chris's kit list for a recent long hike on the Pacific Northwest Trail was a real boon, containing as it did all the latest gear around. He was also extremely helpful when I e-mailed him a number of specific kit queries. There is probably no person in the world who knows more about the latest outdoor kit and which of that kit would be best suited to hiking the Arizona Trail.

Uppermost in my mind was always weight and I managed to squeeze the loaded weight of my pack down to no more than about 20lb, which was very acceptable. The trouble is that having agonised over each and every piece of kit to shave ounces of my pack weight, in would go food for a week and up to a gallon of water, so it often weighed substantially more than 30lb.

Partly because I am completely hopeless with gadgets but mostly because I thought that I might feel more at one with my surroundings, I deliberately shunned technology for the trail. All I carried with me were my SPOT for safety, a very lightweight Kindle and a tiny camera and camcorder. Besides, I believe that the world's trails are now full of people who go to extraordinary lengths to get their pack weight as low as possible and then at the last minute fill it up with half a ton of rattling electronic goods.

I also had to think about the terrain and how rocky it was. Those of you who have been paying attention so far will know that I failed dismally to take that into account as far as my boots were concerned but for other things such as water bottles and sleeping mats, I did manage to get things pretty much right. Altogether, I finished the trail very happy with nearly all my kit choices. Everything except for a couple of pairs of sunglasses made it to the end and it is all intact and ready to go again whenever Mrs B gives me my next pink ticket. This is what I carried with me:-

Pack - Golite seemed to make the best lightweight packs. But after Chris Townsend's Golite Pinnacle collapsed on him in the middle of nowhere on the Pacific Northwest Trail, I chose the slightly sturdier Golite Quest which weighed in at just over 3lb. It proved to be extremely comfortable and durable with pockets in all the right places. I particularly liked the side netting which held my water bottles well and the top pocket from which I could access things that I might need on the trail during the day. The stiff frame and padded back meant that I wasn't bothered at all with kit poking into my back.

Shelter - There are now some fantastic lightweight tents available but I opted for one made by the small American manufacturer, Henry Shires, who with a name like that should probably be making English shooting tweeds. I bought a Henry Shires Contrail Tarptent second hand for £90 and it was worth every penny, weighing in at not much more than 2lbs including pegs and with plenty of space for me and all my gear. One of my Pacer Poles doubled as a tent pole. Mostly it stayed up even in the wind, although during one particularly windy night I took it down and slept on top of it and after that found that I preferred sleeping under the stars, so I mostly used it as a giant groundsheet thereafter.

Sleeping bag and mat – My bag was the one item I got a bit wrong. The night time temperature seldom failed to drop below freezing, often by some distance and the RAB Neutrino 400 that I carefully selected proved not to be thick enough to keep me warm. Most nights I was not as warm as I would have liked and I should have opted for the 600, which would have given me plenty of warmth for just a few extra ounces. For a mat I strapped to the outside of my pack a very clever Pacific Crest Hyper-Lite foam mat which features a body-shaped insert which you blow up to get a little extra cushioning. It was surprisingly comfortable. A proper inflatable mat would probably have punctured in the desert from sharp rocks or cactus thorns.

Cooking stove and kitchen stuff - My cooking stove was a Ti-Tri Inferno, a dual fuel stove easily assembled from a few thin sheets of titanium and weighing only a few ounces. It would take either wood or cooking fuel. The latter, unlike say methylated spirits in England, proved not to be easily available in America except in quantities large enough to burn down a medium-sized apartment block, so I mostly used whatever small sticks I could collect near my campsite. If I made a decent fire, which wasn't a given, I could boil water in about five minutes. I also carried a small titanium pot for boiling water and a plastic mug, both of which were useful for packing small items in my pack, and a spork (combined spoon and fork).

Water containers – I picked up two sturdy one quart Nalgene bottles at a sports shop in Apache Junction and they were just the job. Their wide tops made catching water and stirring it with the Steripen quite easy. I also carried a couple of Platypus bottles, amazingly light and collapsible, but found that I only used them a couple of times at the beginning of the trip. If I was going into a really dry area I would just strap a supermarket half gallon plastic drinks container to the back of my pack. I have already talked about the virtues of the Steripen but in case you weren't paying attention, I used it to sterilise most of my water and carried some tiny Oasis tablets for back-up or to use if the water looked really murky.

195

Footwear – I started the trail with a pair of Hoka One One boots, which I had carefully selected for their comfort and because they helped with an Achilles problem I had been struggling with for a while. Hoka no longer make hiking boots but they still make excellent running shoes which are very popular with ultra distance runners for their immensely thick cushioning. My footwear problems don't need repeating here, assuming you haven't started at the end of the book, as the Chinese do. Before I started out I had been a little too easily seduced by articles extolling the virtues of lightweight boots. I now believe that comfort and durability are more important than shaving a few ounces off your boot weight. For socks I wore some medium weight Bridgedale Trekkers and really appreciated the extra cushioning they provided. I also sprayed everything with a foot odour spray at each resupply town. That kept at bay the smelly feet that can make sharing a tent on the trail with your own footwear quite unpleasant. I carried an extra pair of socks and a small pot of Vaseline to rub on my feet twice a day – it was brilliant for keeping blisters away and to stop my feet drying out in the desert.

Trail Clothing – My trail clothing was all a bit random. I found a pair of North Face shorts in a Holt charity shop and a pair of Mountain Hardwear long trousers online at a good price. Both were very lightweight and very comfortable and the long trousers proved invaluable both in the prickly scrub of the first half of the trail and the snow later on. A trail shirt was surprisingly difficult to find in the middle of the British winter but I stumbled on a Craghoppers trail shirt in the winter sale at my local Norfolk department store, Bakers and Larners of Holt. It was just the job, drying well at the end of each day and I particularly liked the sleeves which you could roll up and then do up some buttons to stop them coming down again. For underwear I wore Finisterre's excellent merino wool pants and carried a spare pair as well, you will be glad to know. They were very hard wearing and extremely comfortable too. I also carried some RAB gloves, a bandana, a fleece beanie and an odd looking sun hat with flaps at the back left over from the Badwater Ultra in Death Valley many years ago. I also carried a lightweight Nike waterproof which I only ever used as extra warmth on one or two exceptionally cold nights. I didn't carry waterproof trousers.

Camp clothing – As soon as I had emptied my pack each evening I would change into some warm gear for camp and with the extremely cold nights I was very glad of it all. First things on were Finisterre merino wool long johns and long sleeved top. As with the Finisterre underpants I found them ideal and for someone who can't normally wear wool anywhere near their body, they gave me no problems with itchy skin. Next on would go PHD (Pete Hutchinson Designs) down trousers and jacket, amazingly lightweight, very warm and packing up into tiny stuff sacs. Finally I carried some thick fleece socks and Outdoordesigns down slippers – the latter were absolutely brilliant, really comfortable to wear and with just enough of a sole to allow me to walk around camp. Most nights I slept in all that gear, including the slippers, often adding a beanie and gloves as well.

Food - Trail food needs to be both lightweight and nourishing but the selection in the resupply towns was often quite limited. Most days started with a couple of packets of porridge and a cup of coffee with milk powder, at lunchtime trail mix or a trail bar and then in the evening noodles or rice, not unlike Pot Noodles in Britain, followed by another trail bar. Not all that thrilling but easy to prepare and it seemed to do me no harm at all. In terms of calories it was nowhere near enough but it did seem to contain enough carbohydrate to sustain my effort. At home I try to eat a really good diet of fresh produce and take whole handfuls of vitamin, herb and mineral supplements but after six weeks of trail food and American breakfasts, burgers and Mexican food in the towns, I wondered why I bothered. I have never felt healthier than I did at the end of the Arizona Trail.

Camera – I carried two very light and inexpensive pieces of equipment with me and a couple of extra memory cards. Chargers went in the post box and so I was able to recharge camera batteries and Kindle at each resupply town. My camera was a Panasonic Lumix DMC-FS15, small enough to carry in my trouser pockets so I was able to snap away whenever I saw a nice view, which means that I have too many pictures of big, open scenery and not enough else! My camcorder is also a Panasonic, an HDC-SD40, extremely light-weight and versatile. So that I could take pictures of myself, I carried a Gorrilapod, a little flexible tripod which you can attach to a rock or branch.

Various bits and pieces – All sorts of odds and sods found their way into the pack and everything went into a selection of neat and waterproof bags in a useful variety of colours, predominantly made by Granite Gear. Most of it was essential but one or two things were just for amusement in the evenings. Pretty much everything was carefully selected to weigh as little as possible. The essentials included my SPOT, a Petzl Tikka headtorch, Black Diamond camp light and spare batteries, very minimal first aid kit and gear repair kit, mini Swiss Army knife, Brunton monocular, waterproof matches, Steripen Adventurer, sunglasses, plastic trowel, mini toothbrush, toothpaste, sunscreen and Vaseline, loo paper and wipes. (American shops sell all sorts of things like toothpaste and sunscreen in very small sizes, ideal for taking on the trail). The luxuries included a large Moleskine notebook and Fisher Space Pen, a Kindle and a paperback, usually picked up in a resupply town library shop, maps and trail notes, an Audobon Natural History Guide and Chris Townsend's Crossing Arizona. With maps, trail notes and excerpts from Crossing Arizona, I only carried the parts relevant to the section I was walking – the rest went ahead in my post box. The final luxury was a pack of 20 cigarettes – smoking a couple at the end of a long day was always a great treat.

CHARITIES, CONTACTING ME
AND OTHER USEFUL INFO

Charities

I walked the Arizona Trail for the sense of achievement, not as a charity thing but I did manage to raise a little money for a couple of really good causes. I paid all my own costs and so everything raised went to my two chosen charities, about £3,500 in all. Thank you to everyone who contributed. Both are still in need of funds but the Just Giving Page set up to make donating easier has been closed. If you have read my book and want to donate anything, you can always send a good old fashioned cheque to me at Holly Lodge. Details of Holly Lodge can be found later in this section.

The charities are:-

1.   **Edith Creasey.** Edith is the daughter of my friends, Ruth and Sean Creasey. She is a very bright and lively five year old from North Norfolk but suffers from cerebral palsy. Her parents desperately need to keep raising funds for her ongoing remedial physical care. There is much that can be done to help with improving her movement but it is highly specialised and costs them a great deal of money. If you Google "Edith Creasey" you can find out a little more but don't donate through the Just Giving pages, they are not current. You can make out a cheque to **Ruth Creasey** and send it to me.

2.   **St Andrew's Church, Thursford.** The lovely Victorian church in my little Norfolk village needs a new roof and new electrics so that the village can continue to use it. We are working hard to raise funds to preserve the building for future generations. You can

find more information on the village website at www.thursford.org and if you feel moved to help, please make out a cheque to **Friends of St Andrew's**.

Holly Lodge and contacting me

I am more than happy to answer any questions you may have about the book, the Arizona Trail or anything else. You can contact me through the website for my North Norfolk B&B, www.hollylodgeguesthouse.co.uk and you will also find my address and contact number there as well. If you want to sell me anything, send me SPAM e-mails or involve me in some dodgy scam to do with huge sums of money allegedly coming from Nigeria, then I don't want to hear from you. We all get quite enough of that sort of thing.

Arizona Trail Association

The Arizona Trail Association is the best place to go to for information on the trail. Their website is really comprehensive and I was in contact with several incredible people at the ATA in the months before I left England. Everyone was amazingly helpful and I could not have completed the journey without the reams of trail notes I downloaded from their website. They have a membership scheme and if you are planning to walk the trail, although you don't have to it is a good idea to join. Hiking the Arizona Trail is of course completely free, which is one of the best things about walking in general.

If I was bit harsh about the trail at times, then I apologise to the ATA. I wrote my diary each evening and so whenever I criticised the trail, it was just the way I was feeling at the time. I do understand how difficult it must be to maintain 800 miles of remote trail with limited resources and a volunteer workforce. Mostly the Arizona Trail is pretty well kept and where it is not, I suppose that all adds to the fun and the challenge.

Suppliers and kit

Sadly I was not sponsored by any kit manufacturers or suppliers but I have already written about the kit I took with me, most of which was fantastic.

These companies stand out for their service, product or company ethos:-
1.   ULTRALIGHTOUTDOORGEAR – Their Teeside showrooms are one the best places in Britain for lightweight hiking gear.
2.   PACER POLES – Their walking poles are probably the best in the world and they were fantastically helpful when I lost part of one of my poles and e-mailed them in the Lake District.
3.   FINISTERRE – A small Cornwall company who are quietly producing some of the best outdoor gear around.
4.   HENRY SHIRES – Their tents are the most amazingly well designed products you will ever find.
5.   PHD – Pete Hutchinson Designs down kit is superb. I wish I had taken one of their sleeping bags as well as a down suit.

Next up

All being well, there might be another adventure in the next year or so and who knows, if anyone buys this one, maybe another book!

19669662R00112

Made in the USA
Charleston, SC
06 June 2013